What Color Is Your Hoodie?

ESSAYS ON BLACK GAY IDENTITY

In thirteen candid and provocative essays, author Jarrett Neal reports on the status of black gay men in the new millennium, examining classism among black gay men, racism within the gay community, representations of the black male body within gay pornography, and patriarchal threats to the survival of both black men and gay men. *What Color Is Your Hoodie?* employs the author's own quest for visibility—through bodybuilding, creative writing, and teaching, among other pursuits—as the genesis for an insightful and critical dialogue that ultimately symbolizes the entire black gay community's struggle for recognition and survival.

"Jarrett Neal's thoughtful and entertaining essays hold a peculiar beauty for those black folks in the know, those not in the know, and in many ways don't want to know. *What Color Is Your Hoodie?* is Baldwinesque in its bareheaded honesty, and this fact alone is worth the price of the ticket."
—Steven G. Fullwood, Co-Editor, *Black Gay Genius: Answering Joseph Beam's Call*

What Color Is Your Hoodie?

ESSAYS ON BLACK GAY IDENTITY

Jarrett Neal

CHELSEA STATION EDITIONS

NEW YORK

What Color Is Your Hoodie?
Essays on Black Gay Identity
by Jarrett Neal

Copyright © 2015 by Jarrett Neal.

All rights reserved.

No part of this book may be reproduced in any form without written permission from the publisher, except by a reviewer, who may quote brief passages in a review where appropriate credit is given; nor may any part of this book be reproduced, stored in a retrieval system, or transmitted in any form or by any means—electronic, photocopying, recording, or other—without specific written permission from the publisher.

These essays are the product of the author's recollections and are thus rendered as a subjective accounting of events that occurred in his life.

Cover art and book design by Peachboy Distillery & Designs
Cover image from Shutterstock.com

Published by Chelsea Station Editions
362 West 36th Street, Suite 2R
New York, NY 10018
www.chelseastationeditions.com
info@chelseastationeditions.com

Paperback ISBN: 978-1-937627-22-5
Ebook ISBN: 978-1-937627-56-0
Library of Congress Control Number: 2015941694

For black gay men everywhere.
All means all.

Contents

Guys and Dolls	11
Weights and Measures	17
Let's Talk About Interracial Porn	45
My Last Love Affair	57
Film Studies for Black Gay Men	63
Teaching Black, Living Gay	75
Baldwin Boys and Harris Homies	95
The Park Bench Promise	109
Real Compared to What	115
Sam I Am	125
Peewee's Peepee	131
What Color is Your Hoodie?	151
Our Fierce Community	167

What Color Is Your Hoodie?

Guys and Dolls

Coach Walker was the first man I ever saw completely naked. I was in eighth grade at the time, and I was miserable. My mother was about to marry a man I didn't particularly like, and after the wedding she and my future stepfather planned to move to Omaha, Nebraska, leaving me behind in Kansas City with my grandparents. At school my classes were either so easy that I found them insulting or so difficult that the low grades I made convinced me I was an idiot. I didn't have cool clothes. I didn't have a girlfriend. My complete lack of athletic ability excluded me from the popular group of boys, the ones who hooted and hollered in the back of the school bus; the ones, who, at fourteen, already possessed the brawny, robust physiques of full grown men; whose laughter peeled from the mischief they caused and the misery they inflicted. This, I later assumed, was one of the reasons our school didn't force students to shower after gym class. Packs of rowdy pubescent boys given running water, towels, and permission to remove their clothes—boys fascinated with all things sexual and imbued with the rampant homophobia that codifies their behavior well into manhood—augured nothing less than disaster, and our principal wanted to avoid it. Our junior high school employed three gym teachers: Coach Smith, a tiny African American woman who taught girls PE; my gym teacher, Coach Manning, a man so overweight he could be heard wheezing from several feet away; and Coach Walker, a brash and brawny young African American man with sandy hair, honey skin, and a goatee. He roughhoused with the boys and was every girl's fantasy.

In college he had excelled at virtually every sport, and the proof of his athleticism, a physique stacked head to foot and front to back with bulging hard muscles, was unquestionable. Coach Walker was the only teacher who got away with cussing at us and telling us dirty jokes. He zoomed through the school's parking lot in a black Corvette while NWA quaked his speakers. To my classmates and I, Coach Walker put the kool in Kool Aid, and we were as mortified as him when we filed into the locker room after spending gym period outside playing football and happened upon him naked in the communal showers. The sight of him stark naked inspired a rowdy response from most of the boys, yet stunned silence from me and a couple of my peers. Seeing Coach Walker standing under the steamy shower that autumn afternoon, his golden brown body glistening, his tumescent penis bouncing from one tree trunk thigh to the other, ended my boyhood. I never knew anyone could be so beautiful, certainly not a man, a naked man. It was like watching one of my action figures come to life.

Two years earlier, when I was a small boy in elementary school, *He-Man and the Masters of the Universe* was the most popular cartoon among boys. I raced home every day after school to watch timid yet herculean Prince Adam extend his long, heavy Sword of Power, shout, "By the power of Grayskull!" and magically transform into He-Man, the half-naked blond, bronzed barbarian who defended the planet Eternia from Skeletor and other half-naked barbarians (with such blatant homoerotic imagery, Mattel can probably take more than a little credit for captivating an entire generation of gay men). My mother bought me a new Masters of the Universe action figure each payday and when I played with them my imagination soared. Eventually I amassed a collection of action figures so large that there wasn't one character on the cartoon I didn't have a figure for. Castle Grayskull itself, a three-foot high plastic structure colored green and made to look as ghoulish and ferocious as the castle on the cartoon, was the bulwark of my collection. My mother gave it to me for Christmas. Three months later I turned twelve and decided I was too old to play with toys, so I packed up all of my action figures and dumped them into the trash

What Color Is Your Hoodie?

along with Castle Grayskull. Mama went berserk.

We call them action figures: miniature plastic replicas of superheroes marketed to little boys. And boys love them. I recall spending countless hours of my boyhood running, jumping and stomping all over my grandparents' house with my action figures, lowering my voice when I spoke for them and imaging storylines that were much more complex than the ones I saw on the cartoon each afternoon. In this regard action figure seems to be the most appropriate term for these toys. Yet the language our culture uses to describe these figures reveals our own anxiety regarding masculinity. They're dolls. We know this. Yet the cultural fear that boys who play with dolls become sissies demands that we rename them. I wasn't the only boy who enjoyed playing with action figures and I doubt I was the only boy whose sexuality quite literally sprung to life when we packed into the locker room too early and surprised Coach Walker in all his naked beauty. Many of my classmates cackled and pointed; some even whistled. Embarrassed, Coach Walker snatched his towel from the hook just outside the communal showers and barked, "Get dressed!" He boomed the same words over and over as if the thunder of his voice and the repetition of the words themselves, like Prince Adam's magical invocation, would be enough to enrobe him, to eradicate the image of his body, and the diversity of feelings he inspired, from our crude adolescent minds. How could we be comfortable with nudity when we were forbidden to disrobe and bathe in front of each other? Our only model for manhood, in one mortifying incident, had been made human and all too fallible.

Men were scarce in the environment I grew up in. There's an old joke about Father's Day in the ghetto. The punch line: What's Father's Day? As tasteless as the joke is it underscores the reality of boyhood for untold numbers of African American boys who, like me, had no male role models. Our mothers, almost in desperation, relied on He-Man among other superheroes and action film stars, toys and games, sports and social interactions, to fill the void left by our absent fathers. They were poor substitutes, yet a starving child can transform cracker crumbs into a banquet. I took great pleasure in the hours I spent playing with my action figures. Indeed I, like so many of my creative peers, credit playtime with cultivating my imagination and providing the genesis of my desire to write. Happy in my world of make believe, He-Man and his ilk allowed me to become anyone and do anything I wished, whether it was battling Skeletor or riding Battle Cat through the untamed wilderness of Eternia. Yet at no time during these play sessions or my pubescent years did it ever occur to me that He-man was an undeniable stud. Mattel, the company that created not only the Masters of the Universe line of toys and games but also the thirty-minute animated series, states in his biography that He-Man stands six feet two inches tall and weighs around two hundred and twenty-five pounds. But anyone with keen eyesight knows that these measurements, like the character himself, are utter fiction. Wimpy boys like me could only dream of attaining the physicality and confidence He-Man, a veritable muscle god, possessed. The daily taunts from my peers and the ache of fatherlessness, an absence I feel even as an adult, crippled my sense of self-worth. Like He-Man's alter ego Prince Adam, I scarcely knew what to do with myself. I needed to become He-Man just as much as he did.

A man with the body of a gladiator walks through a fantastical world populated by anthropomorphic creatures, robots, warriors, and sorceresses, wearing only jack boots, a furry brown Speedo, and a metal harness that bears a flaming Iron Cross. His muscles are swollen to outrageous proportions, striated and pumped, resembling an archetype of masculinity found, in the real world, only on the covers of bodybuilding magazines. This is He-Man—perhaps the single most striking and iconic image of my boyhood. Introduced to boys in the mid-1980s, He-Man represented the nation's "bigger is better" zeitgeist: a decade when Americans were trouncing competitors in the Olympics, in the nuclear arms race and on the silver screen. Arnold Schwarzenegger, Jean Claude Van Damme, and Sylvester Stallone were knocking down doors and kicking in dicks in a string of action flicks that capitalized on their steroid-pumped bodies and athletic prowess. Coach Walker, with his hunky sculpted physique, hairy chest, and husky drill sergeant's voice, could easily have taken a place beside these box office

What Color Is Your Hoodie?

behemoths. In the fleeting moments I watched him step out of the shower, grab his white towel and bound into his office twenty feet away, my own Sword of Power joust the air. Though my classmates and I had come upon Coach Walker by surprise, catching him in the most exposed and vulnerable situation a person can find himself in, at no time after the incident did any of us think less of him. He scared and fascinated us before we saw him naked and wet, and he continued to exude charisma and strength in the months and weeks that followed. This, I think, makes muscle men so appealing—their ability to simultaneously arouse and terrify, to meld brutality and fear with beauty and sensuality, inhabiting the roles of father, hero, lover and disciplinarian.

I didn't acknowledge my sexual attraction to men until my freshman year of college. Four more years passed before I gained the courage to admit to myself that I am gay. These years were marked by anger, frustration, fear, despair and, most of all, loneliness. Yet with maturity comes perspective and wisdom, the ability to sort out the past and find solace in truth. I would have given anything to be as powerful as He-Man or as attractive as Coach Walker but one was a cartoon, the other was a man, and I mythologized both of them. They gave me comfort and amusement and taught me many lessons in their own ways. The most valuable lesson of all was to save myself, be my own hero and gather strength from within. Still, I wish I had kept those action figures. They might be worth a lot of money today.

Weights and Measures

One

In elementary school, probably third grade, my classmates and I were allowed to participate in afterschool extracurricular activities, among them basketball and arts and crafts. I had zero interest in basketball: not only did I lack athletic ability, boys didn't like to play with me because I was soft, a nerd. I opted for arts and crafts, and after my mother signed the permissions slip I joined Mrs. Bible (who would become my teacher two years later) and nine girls in the school's cafeteria. We spent our time gluing construction paper into abstract creations and making bizarre sculptures with popsicle sticks and uncooked elbow macaroni. I fancied myself a future Picasso or Pollack, men who, I wouldn't learn until much later in life, exuded masculinity while creating some of the most beautiful works of art the world has even known. Many black folks in the ghetto simply couldn't comprehend men devoting themselves to painting and sculpting; artistic pursuits were for white boys and black men who were *that* way. I can't help thinking now that if they had known about Palmer Hayden, Archibald Motley, Jean-Michel Basquiat and so many others, their thinking and, by grand extension, their circumstances would have been different. After attending two arts and crafts sessions, Mrs. Bible took me aside and gently asked, "Wouldn't you like to play basketball with the other boys? Arts and crafts is more for girls." She escorted me up to the gym and spoke with the coach, Mr. Beets. I stood at the gym's entrance and watched them talking on the edge of the basketball court. Mrs. Bible spoke with her slender arms wrapped around her delicate frame while Mr.

Beets scratched his fiery red beard and nodded. From time to time they would glance at me. When she left I joined four other sissies on the bleachers; Mr. Beets asked us to spend some time watching the other boys play so we would understand the game. None of them wanted us to play and we, the sissies, all knew this. I snuck out of the gym before practice was over and never returned. This experience may have skewed my perception of both athletics and painting, yet I didn't need to be Michael Jordan or Rodin to accomplish the task I would embark on with plain glue and glitter when I was twenty years old.

    I drove to Walgreens and bought a poster-sized sheet of black construction paper, Elmer's glue, and two bottles of glitter: one blue, the other red. When I got home I locked myself in my bedroom, scrawled out words on the paper with the glue then poured equal amounts of the blue and red glitter over it. Once the glue dried I tacked the poster high on the wall opposite my bed so that every morning when I woke and every night before I went to sleep I would read the motivational message on it, take the words to heart, and reach my goal. I had read somewhere that a goal written down and read aloud each day was a goal one would be more likely to achieve. I hoped this was true. The sign, because of the glitter, sparkled even in the dark, so that if I awakened in the middle of the night just briefly I would see the message and strengthen my commitment to my goal: GET BIGGER!

* * *

Our family made fun of my mother when she decided to stop eating red meat. As a part-time model with the John Casablancas Agency in Kansas City (the agency that would represent me during my laughably short career as a model when I was nineteen), Mother was a fitness enthusiast. It was the mid-1980s and all across the country women were stepping into leotards and leg warmers, popping *The Jane Fonda Workout* into their VCRs and getting physical. Mother rose at six every morning, turned on the television and bounced around the living room to *The 20 Minute Workout*, kicking and

What Color Is Your Hoodie?

punching at the air with the fury of a woman being attacked by muggers. She jogged through Loose Park with five pound weights strapped to her ankles, popped amino acids as if they were jellybeans, dined on leafy salads and mineral water. And it paid off. My mother booked steady modeling gigs during the Eighties, both runway and print, and even opened a women's gym, Derriere's, long before Curves launched in the mid-1990s.

Before she owned her own gym she worked out at Gold's in Overland Park, Kansas. Once, she took me along to the gym with her. Though I was only eleven I knew quite a bit about exercise and fitness from my mother and special programs I had taken part in at school like Jump Rope for Heart. I was well aware which foods lacked proper nutrition and which would help me build strong bones and keep me healthy. I knew that the cardiovascular exercises my mother did were beneficial, yet I had no idea what it took for men to become herculean like Arnold Schwarzenegger and my hero, He-Man. I wandered the gym while my mother took an aerobics class, careful not to get in anyone's way or meddle with any of the equipment. A few people smiled at me and said hello. I was struck by the cacophony of the place: good Eighties pop music (this was the first place I ever heard Madonna: "Borderline"), the sharp clang of metal against metal, men moaning, grunting and shouting in agony. It all seemed so easy yet, from the sounds they were making and the strained expressions in their faces, painful beyond words. Mother's twenty minute workout left her looking invigorated and energized. After hefting massive pounds, these men looked ready to collapse.

When Mother finished her class she and a girlfriend were strength training on Nautilus machines. I pointed to the free weight area, populated by men with gladiatorial physiques, and asked, "Why don't you work out in there?"

She rose from the bench, wiped her forehead with the back of her hand and said, "In there? Those guys will intimidate the hell out of you."

It was the first time I had ever heard her swear.

* * *

During my freshman year at Northwestern University I tried to get into the habit of going to the gym and eating healthfully. My roommate Roger, a six foot two corn-fed white boy from downstate Illinois whose only interests in life were football and big titties, was a regular gym rat, spending any free time he had at Patten Gymnasium, a decades-old gym with no windows where all the football players and bodybuilders swung around eighty-pound dumbbells like they were foam pillows. I opted to work out at the Sports Pavilion and Aquatic Center, commonly called SPAC, a relatively new facility on campus that offered high end amenities including a lap pool, handball and tennis courts, saunas, hot tubs, and a sports bar. I didn't have a plan in mind when I went to the gym. I avoided free weights, committing myself to working out on Nautilus equipment and stopping only when my muscles began to hurt. I never asked Roger for guidance or work out tips because I was too embarrassed. Besides, I had heard him make derisive comments to friends about guys at the gym who weren't truly committed to pumping iron, and I didn't want to be added to his list of also-rans.

When I had been placed on academic leave at the close of the school year, I returned to my bedroom in my grandmother's house and began to grow my own small gym. I started with a barbell and a set of sand-filled plates my mother had passed along to me. I had precious little space and no idea of what to do to transform my physique, but Mother helped me. She told me that I should concentrate on three exercises: squats, deadlifts, and bench presses. I could manage the first two exercises but I had no hard flat surface in my bedroom that would allow me to perform barbell presses. I improvised and did them flat on my back on the floor. Every other night around nine o'clock I shut my bedroom door, turned on some pop music, and lifted as much weight as I could, and for a while I was successful, seeing marked results in my size and muscle tone, particularly in my quads.

Working out at home was cheaper than joining a gym, and within the solitude of my own room the wrenching feelings of inadequacy I experienced each time I entered a gym were temporarily allayed. Once I got a job in the mailroom of an insurance company I earned

What Color Is Your Hoodie?

enough money to invest in a set of cast iron hexagonal dumbbells ranging in weight from ten pounds to fifty pounds. Several months earlier Mother had purchased me a home gym machine for Christmas, an outsize apparatus that allows one to perform the most essential exercises: incline and flat bench press, lying leg extension, preacher curls, lat pulldowns, and seated leg curls. With the addition of my dumbbells and a weight belt I was well equipped to achieve my fitness goals.

Space, however, was still a problem. Our single-level home had no basement and no garage. The only extra space was the small shed behind the house and it was packed with furniture, boxes of decorations and photographs, memorabilia, and other odds and ends. My bedroom was the only place I could exercise. So whenever I worked out I took my worn queen sized bed, mattress, frame and all, lifted it on its side and pushed it flush against the wall. Yet these efforts had the opposite effect. While I was committed to working out for a few months, eventually I slacked off. My weights and equipment became covered with a patina of dust. I realize now that the major problem with exercising at home is that it belies our primal understanding of what a home should be: a place of comfort, relaxation, and renewal. While others may find great success exercising in the privacy of their home, I need my home to be a refuge, a place where I escape all stress and anxiety. The pent-up negative emotions we release during workouts secrete into the atmosphere. At the gym, I believe, those charged emotions are cleansed and recycled among other people working out and motivates them, for example, to run another mile on the treadmill or force out two more reps on the lat pulldown. One can never fully divest those bad feelings when working out at home, where they hover and eventually absorb into the walls, the furniture and every fixture. It isn't surprising to me now that during the time I was exercising in my bedroom not only did I suffer from depression but I also began to experience insomnia. I continue to struggle with these conditions periodically all these years later.

In my twenties the gym represented myriad conflicting ideas to me, reflective of the conflicts within myself at the time. Confused about my sexual orientation, my participation (or lack of it) in university studies, my prospects for a career, my relationships with family, friends, and the world around me, I could not attend to my body's needs when my emotions were so off kilter. While many men in their early twenties quickly learn to utilize the gym as an arena to battle their demons, sculpt their bodies, burn off excess energy, and keep their natural aggression in check, it would be many years before I learned to utilize the gym in the same way. Sullen and remote, the gym, for me, was heavenhell, alternately a torture chamber and a sanctuary, an erotic space and a storehouse of shame. No place could make me feel as gangly, weak, and inadequate as a men's locker room. Conversely, no place surged my lust quite like men's locker rooms, populated, as they so often are, with an alluring crush of men moving throughout the space in varying states of undress, their faces flushed, their muscles pumped, the odor from their sweat-glazed bodies potently arousing. Most gay men, I am sure, can relate to the complex feelings I encountered each time I entered the men's locker room: the desire to ogle men as they dress and undress, and the fear of being caught looking; the joy of being recognized for your own beauty and the agony of going unnoticed. The paradox of being surrounded by objects of lust yet denied access to them compounded my ambivalence over my sexuality but at the same time it spurred my quest to achieve the Adonis physique I had coveted for the better part of my life.

At every gym I have ever belonged to the men bearing the most muscle are the men who garner the most attention, admiration, and respect from other muscle disciples. The Hercules with the thirty-two inch waist, twenty-four inch biceps, meaty thighs, and a flawless V-taper is the man I and so many other gay men both desire and envy. That gay men historically have been likened to Narcissus, the pulchritudinous youth in Greek mythology who, loving himself so much, drowned in a pool reflecting his own image when he attempted to kiss it, is not surprising. The concept of the gay clone originates from this myth: gay men who spend a considerable amount of time and money trying to look as close to physical perfection as they can; who spend long hours at the gym each week pumping iron,

What Color Is Your Hoodie?

sprinting on treadmills, performing crunches, and sweltering in saunas; who go into debt buying just the right designer clothes and wearing them in just the right way; who seek the exclusive company of men who are their perfect match in every respect, physically, socially, and financially. It is because of the gay clone and for entry into his society that so many gay men like me have placed our physical, emotional and financial health at risk. Even before I was aware of my homosexuality I knew that if I was ever to be included among the most brilliant and successful members of society I had to alter myself in aggregate ways. Day after day I would go to the gym and flounder in my attempt to achieve the same impressive titan physique so many other men at my gym possessed. I assumed I had bad genes or that the men I envied and lusted after were using steroids or performance enhancing drugs (undoubtedly, as I would come to learn over the years, many were). I wasn't motivated enough, I thought. I wasn't really trying. I continually suffered sore muscles, so sore in fact that some days walking from my bedroom to the bathroom in the morning proved an agonizing experience. And for all of the hours I spent haphazardly exercising I had made no real progress toward achieving the body I wanted and the acceptance, from myself and others, I believed would come from developing a hunky physique.

When I turned twenty-seven, however, my thoughts changed. I began to take stock of the situation. I had a fully paid gym membership, a job that paid me enough money to buy the healthy foods and supplements I needed to bulk up, no other time commitments, and no other responsibilities. Most of all, I was educated and intelligent, much more intelligent than the lunkheads who spent half their day banging weights in the gym and the other half channeling surfing on their mommy's couch. There was no reason I couldn't achieve the same muscularity and physicality as these men, so being the nerd that I am I did what most nerds do: I studied. I bought *Muscle & Fitness* every month and read it from cover to cover, and when I went to the gym I would mimic routines of the various professional bodybuilders printed within the glossy pictorial's pages. I became a spy at the gym, making mental notes of the exercises, sets and reps performed by each of the men whose bodies I admired. I learned all I could about bodybuilding supplements: which would make me bigger and firmer, which would burn fat, which brands were most effective and which, with their proprietary blends, were junk. My diet changed: chicken breasts, brown rice, and steamed broccoli became the standard meal in our household, and even today my husband Gerald and I dine on some version of it at least once a week. Had I truly been enrolled in a course in health and fitness there is no doubt I would have earned an A. As I spent more money on supplements and purchased more bodybuilding books and magazines, kept a workout diary and paid careful attention to the exercises other men in the gym were performing—the pounds they were lifting, the number of repetitions, the length of rest breaks—my body responded. After weeks of consistent weightlifting and adhering to a proper diet, my shirts became tighter and the weights I had been lifting felt lighter. The denizens of the gym were beginning to notice me as well. After spending so many years of my life languishing in invisibility, men in the gym had begun to acknowledge me, to nod hello and even ask me to spot them, a sure sign, in the unspoken vernacular of all gyms, that I had become one of the more experienced and admired members of the community. It had all worked.

    I'll never forget my first trip back to Kansas City after intensifying my workout routine. I hadn't seen my relatives in many months. My mother and grandmother, along with an aunt and two cousins, were sitting on the front porch of my grandmother's house awaiting my arrival. When I stepped out of the car dressed in jeans and a snug T-shirt, their shouts of awe and disbelief at the sight of my bulked up torso, arms, and shoulders proved that I had indeed achieved my fitness goals. Yet for all the praise my new body earned me, in spite of the men who cruised me on the street and my husband's amorous attentions, I still hadn't achieved the herculean physique I knew I could only acquire by using steroids, a measure I couldn't bring myself to take. Though I had achieved the goal of getting bigger, in my mind I was still a scrawny wimp.

    The Adonis Complex is a book I discovered a couple of months

What Color Is Your Hoodie?

after Gerald and I moved from Kansas City to Chicago in the fall of 1999. A clinical study of body dysmorphia, eating disorders, steroid abuse, and cosmetic surgery among American men at the close of the twentieth century, I purchased the book from Unabridged Books, Chicago's historic LGBT bookstore, and immediately became engrossed in it, recognizing myself on nearly every page of the text. I had come out of the closet three years earlier, and I was unaware of the unrelenting quest for beauty and physical perfection that drives most gay men. It never dawned on me prior to coming out that individuals who engage in sexual relations with men are more concerned with their appearance than individuals who have sex with women, who are far less visually oriented. The relationship we form with our bodies directly expresses the connection we forge between our inner selves and the world around us. This is obvious to psychologists, personal trainers, nutritionists, and the like. But for the rest of us, coming to this realization may take years, even decades. Understanding that beauty is socially constructed proves challenging in Western culture which attaches commerce, power, and privilege to beauty; a culture responsible for the global transmission of beauty and the industries that generate billions of dollars scaring and intimidating hapless consumers into altering themselves to conform to its rigid standards. Still, despite this truth and our informed knowledge of the risks and dangers concomitant with particular diets and supplements—especially steroids—I and other men remain inflexible: transforming ourselves from puny/pudgy beta-males into brawny alpha-males is worth the risk.

Few things in life surpass my ceaseless quest for protein, the cornerstone of a bodybuilding lifestyle. Efforts to seek, find, and consume sufficient amounts of quality protein each day at regular three hour intervals is the mark of a true bodybuilder, along with tendinitis, calloused palms, and a perpetually dirty blender. When, after several months of intense study, I realized that the key to building muscle was nourishing my body with lean protein round the clock, I embarked on an obsessive search for it, stuffing myself beyond the point of satiety so I could digest the required level I needed to maintain mass and build even more muscle. The formula is this: to activate muscle growth, an individual should consume roughly one gram of protein per pound of body weight. Stated plainly, a one hundred and fifty pound man should consume slightly more than one hundred fifty grams of protein each day. This isn't always the easiest of tasks, however. Anyone not a professional bodybuilder or fitness model, anyone who works a standard forty hour work week and strives to maintain close bonds with family and friends is perhaps unaware that acquiring lean protein in a nation that thrives on high calorie energy-dense foods requires a great deal of planning and scheduling. Yet a high protein diet is the foundation of bodybuilding and nothing can substitute for it. In the absence of lean protein, and given the ever-increasing restrictions on my time, my diet lost quality and proportion. I struggled to eat clean each day. I would try to compensate for slacking off during stressful periods at work by making wiser food choices on weekends and vacations, but eventually I began to crave comfort foods on my days off. Sugar is, was, and always will be the kryptonite that imperils my dreams of becoming a Superman. But being young and remaining physically active, I assumed, would protect me from the deleterious effect such lopsided dieting would have on a normal, inactive person.

The most obvious clue that my sloppy diet had compromised my fitness goals revealed itself in my wardrobe. My pants became tighter in the thighs and butt. I had been bodybuilding long enough to know the difference between an increase in muscle mass and an increase in fat, and there was no doubt that the size I was putting on did not belong in the former category but the latter. Initially I attributed this to too many squats and other leg exercises. Owing to genetics, I have always possessed muscular quads and firm, ample buttocks folks in the ghetto would call a badoonkadonk (even as I approach middle age my butt continues to earn me compliments from men and women alike). Yet as time passed, shopping for pants became a frustrating and embarrassing experience for me, as I needed to go up and up in size. Although my waist stayed the same size I simply couldn't fit my thighs and rear into the vast majority of jeans and pants. Coinciding with the fashion industry's turn toward skinny and slim fit jeans and pants, I, like so many other men who

What Color Is Your Hoodie?

possess beefy lower halves—African American men, bodybuilders, and cyclists in particular—was forced to buy my pants one or two sizes too big then have them altered in the waist to fit. Once again I found it necessary to alter my diet and my workout regimen.

Life gets in the way, as it often does when one matures. Mounting work demands, creative pursuits and commitments to my family and friends make eating clean, working out like a demon and sleeping eight to ten hours a night a monumental effort at certain times of the year. I have come to realize, finally, after countless hours spent hating myself for not looking like Hugh Jackman, that the body I have always desired is the body for a man who doesn't live the kind of life I live, a man who, like Hugh Jackman, must earn his living with his body. Actors, models, athletes, and porn stars, the beautiful godlike men gay men so ardently desire, are paid to be muscular and fast, or beautifully sculptured and unobtainable, or sexually voracious. Men who can earn a living doing other things besides tossing a football, acting like a superhero or getting gangbanged by scores of strangers don't need to be visions of male beauty and physical perfection, and even the men who work in such professions do not and cannot maintain their flawless physiques for long. Nothing in life is static, certainly not a human body.

I doubt I will ever stop lifting weights. So long as I maintain my health and have access to a gym I will continue to keep my body conditioned. But it feels good to let go sometimes, to indulge in rich, high calorie comfort foods, sleep late on the weekends and sometimes skip the gym altogether and engage in other activities: strolling through a museum, reading a good book in a coffee shop, brunching with friends. Gym rats like me often forget there is a life to be lived outside the gym, where people eat because food is good, embrace their natural bodies and those of others. I know now that our bodies not only change as we age, our diets change as well and the lives we live beyond the gym require even more care and attention if we desire physical transformation within the gym.

Jarrett Neal

Two

Diesel Washington is on a rant. The African American gay porn star, formerly signed with Titan Media, a juggernaut among gay porn studios, is going off on Marc Dylan, another porn star who recently posted a long YouTube video in which he confessed, in so many words, that he doesn't perform with black men because he isn't attracted to them. Individuals select sexual partners on the basis of many aesthetic preferences, and while lack of erotic interest in a particular group does not necessarily connote racism the complex mix of humans' sexual biases and preferences has origins that are socially and politically constructed. Diesel Washington is certainly no Cornell West or bell hooks, but I applaud him for being the sole voice in gay porn who calls out the industry's obvious racism. In his book *Why I Hate Abercrombie and Fitch*, scholar Dwight McBride criticizes the porn industry and gay culture at large for stigmatizing black men:

> Operating on many of the most readily imaginable stereotypes about black masculinity, [gay pornographic] films do not disappoint viewers who bring to them a desire for a variety of black manhood closely associated with the brutish, the socially and economically disempowered (though never physically or sexually), the violent, and a fantastic insatiable animal sexuality that will fuck you tirelessly and still be ready for more.[1]

The gravamen of McBride's case against homosexual white men points to a diluted brand of racism which has trickled down from a more potent strain that courses through Western culture. As a group which itself endures bigotry, discrimination, violence, and exoticization, homosexuals can empathize with the struggles of African Americans; comparisons between the Civil Rights movement of the 1950s and 1960s and the current Gay Rights movement abound and discriminatory laws against African Americans are commonly cited as precedent for extending

---

1, Dwight A. McBride. *Why I Hate Abercrombie and Fitch: Essays on Race and Sexuality*. (New York: New York University Press, 2005). 102-103.

and protecting rights for the LGBT community. For Black Gay Americans the obvious parallel between these two groups, their histories, aesthetics, traditions, and struggles make us all the more sensitive to injustices felt by these groups, and the fact that Diesel Washington, a renowned sex worker, vocalizes his outrage at the gay porn industry's abuses indicates black gay men's heightened awareness of the ways race and sexuality problematize each other in our society.

Gay men are different from heterosexuals and lesbians in regard to our relationship with pornography. So much more than a frenetic expression of lasciviousness, porn, for gay men, affirms our desires amid a cultural ethos which deems them despicable and teaches us to appreciate our bodies while encouraging us to take pride in our sexual longings. Most importantly, gay porn places the male body on full display, glorifying the male as both an object of sexual desire and a repository of cultural, historic, and aesthetic beauty. Beautiful women abound in Western culture, exhibited in countless ways in countless venues. A beautiful woman puts people at ease; a beautiful man, however, causes unease in people because his beauty forces individuals to consider gender and sex in a different way, to reassess their values, beliefs, and the very structure of patriarchy. Though straight men enjoy numerous mediums that will cater to their aesthetic and sexual desires for women, one of the few places gay men are guaranteed to find gorgeous men who will satisfy their erotic ideations is gay pornography, which belies patriarchal sexuality by broadening the scope of masculine erotic desire to encompass a plurality of sexual expressions, including autoeroticsm, bisexuality, and sadomasochism. Like porn for women, gay porn wrests the erotic gaze from white heterosexual men and places it under the exclusive purview of homosexual men. It is possible for gay porn stars, due to gay adult entertainment's specialized status, to achieve a level of celebrity among gay men that approaches stardom in the mainstream. Thanks to social media, porn stars can attract legions of fans worldwide simply because they provide gay and bisexual men and a few heterosexual woman what the dominant culture cannot—gorgeous men we can objectify and dominate at will.

Standards of beauty in the gay community derive from porn. The men who fuck, cavort, and put their naked bodies on display in these films communicate the types of beauty prized in our community, and disturbingly, the vast majority of these men are white. Studios like Titan Media, Colt Studios. and Falcon Studios, as well as online studios such as Men.com, Men at Play. and Corbin Fisher, showcase scores of handsome, well-built men, yet few of them are of African descent. When Diesel Washington reigned as the premiere black performer at Titan in the late 2000s, the number of black men in the mainstream of gay porn was slim. Washington has expressed on his blog and in interviews that at the beginning of his porn career, agents and producers informed him that he would never appear on a box cover or headline a major studio production, and that the few films he did headline would find an audience primarily in urban (read: black) areas. In the years since Washington's tenure, the number of A-list black men in the industry has declined further with Race Cooper stepping into Diesel Washington's position. Another disturbing trend that began with stars Matthew Rush and Dred Scott is the practice of white-skinned biracial performers being cast alongside the white megastars of gay porn while their true racial and ethnic background is concealed, either by the studios or by the models themselves. Matthew Rush, in interviews after he left Falcon Studios, stated that When he was signed to an exclusive contract with Falcon Studios, he lobbied to perform with other black men but was denied by director Chi Chi LaRue. This practice of "whitewashing" biracial models has continued, with Austin Wilde, Roman Wright, and a few other biracial performers choosing not to acknowledge their African American identity in interviews. Austin Wilde, for his part, recently shot his first scene with a black performer, a decision Wilde made, porn fans claim, to deflect accusations that he is a "snow queen."

Perhaps no human has been studied so often and finds himself at the center of so much cultural and political debate as African and African descended men. Our bodies simultaneously attract and repel white patriarchy and in the world of pornography, both gay and straight, this dichotomy is amplified. The Western world exhibits

What Color Is Your Hoodie?

a somewhat mystical fascination with black men, our bodies, our psychology, our politics, and our aesthetics. Yet our bodies—more to the point, our sexual energies and expressions—animate political, cultural, and academic fervor throughout the West. Everyone, it seems, wants a big black dick. Straight men like to watch women get fucked by one, gay men want to be fucked by one, and we all wish we had one dangling between our legs. The world of pornography is saturated with images of abnormally long, thick black penises that orally, vaginally, and anally penetrate hosts of individuals who have found their way into the X-rated arena. Anyone raised within Western culture is well aware of the sexual stereotypes prescribed to men of African descent. As an African American man, I have a few stories to tell about past lovers, primarily white men, who have unzipped my pants and eagerly anticipated a penis the size of a hot house cucumber to flop out. Endowments aside, black men have a tremendous onus on us to live up to centuries old expectations in regard to our sexual prowess. We have been cast, it seems, as paragons of raw sexual energy: muscled, athletic towers of ebony or brown fuckability who can go and go and go for hours, thrusting deep, probing, stretching, hitting all the good spots, even those the men/women we are servicing didn't know they had. It's a lot to live up to, yet I, and other black men who have written about this topic, aren't quite sure how we should feel about it. Every man wants to be thought of as an expert lover, but when the arc of one's life can be reduced to one's status as a stud, an ability which does nothing to separate man from beast, such monikers degrade rather than compliment.

So as black men mature, educate ourselves, and conduct sexual relationships—intraracial or interracial, heterosexual or homosexual, monogamous or nonmonogamous—inevitably we are confronted with the Mandingo stereotype, forged out of a racist past yet perpetuated by a masculine desire to attain alpha male status, to be the cock of the walk. Cross-racially, sexual conquests serve as a primal declaration of manhood, yet many African American men, denied a broader way in which to express their manhood, "[see] status and economic success as synonymous with endless sexual conquest"[2]. Though we live in a nation led by an African descended man, black men in toto are a long way from acquiring the same space in society their Caucasian counterparts inhabit. Statistically, black men are more likely to be incarcerated and fall into unemployment than white men. Our life expectancy is shorter and our overall standard of living pales in comparison to white men. In spite of the tremendous strides the African American community has made over the last half century, black men are falling farther and farther behind all other groups of men except in the area of sexual desirability.

This takes us back to pornography. Anyone who has spent a considerable amount of time with pornographic images or literature knows that pornography is a low form of art, base and often uninspired. Yet there is great power in porn—indeed, all forms of sexual expression, be they public or private, inspire the consumer to some sort of release or response which manifests in masturbation, mimicry, or outcry. The very first pornographic film I saw was titled *Let Me Tell Ya 'Bout White Chicks*. It was produced by VCA Pictures and released in 1984. I found a VHS copy of it in a relative's home while I, a nosy, precocious teenager, was snooping through his belongings (if he is reading this essay now, please know that I sincerely apologize for invading your privacy and have as much respect and admiration for you as I have always had). Eager and horny kid that I was, I snuck the tape into my backpack and took it home with me. *Let Me Tell Ya 'Bout White Chicks* concerns a group of five African American hooligans who sit around a friend's bedroom one slow evening regaling one another with tales of their sexual conquests with white women. Their aim is to convince their host, a slender chestnut colored black man wearing a multicolored shirt, mustard yellow pants, and a gold medallion around his neck, that white women are sexually gifted and he should try having sex with one. The skeptic is unconvinced until one of the men enlists the services of a buxom red-haired white woman to convert him. Her efforts are successful: as two of his friends watch from the bedside, the skeptic

---

2. bell hooks. *We Real Cool: Black Men and Masculinity* (New York: Ramparts, 2004), 100.

What Color Is Your Hoodie?

fucks her in a variety of positions until he spatters a goodly amount of semen on her lower back. I was a mere adolescent when I first saw this film, barely out of junior high school, yet each scene in the film—except the lesbian three-way—had such a profound impact on me that years later, as an adult man in a stable, loving, sexually monogamous relationship, I discovered the movie on an Internet site and ordered it so I could masturbate to it by myself. The men in this movie were not terrifically endowed; compared to such sizable black men currently working in straight porn—Lexington Steele, Shane Diesel, and Mandingo, for example—the penises of the actors in *Let Me Tell Ya 'Bout White Chicks* were an average size. Yet the experience of seeing men, any men, engaged in sexual intercourse stirred my nascent lust while augmenting my libido and the way I navigate life as a sexual being more than any other form of pornography I've come into contact with since.

Still, the racialized component of *Let Me Tell Ya 'Bout White Chicks*, a film targeted to men—black, white, and others—who lust to witness white women sexually dominated and exploited by men of African descent, cannot be discounted. Like mainstream films, most pornographic films assume a white male gaze. In an interview with author Scott Poulson-Bryant, porn star Lexington Steele explains that "[w]hite consumers have certain expectations... [t]he idea of the big black buck deflowering the little virginal white girl is very popular"[3]. Proof of this claim can be found in any adult video store or on any porn website, where a preponderance of films specializing in black male-white female sexual pairings has made the interracial porn market highly lucrative. The fact that white male-black female sexual pairings in porn are far less common speaks to the viewing population's unease with such pairings given common knowledge of the ugly history of black women raped and sexually exploited by white men during the slave era and Jim Crow. When individuals engage in sexual activity, either alone or with others, we bring culture, history, commerce, politics, and social discourse into the setting with us. The release and exchange of

---

3. Scott Poulson-Bryant. *Hung: A Meditation on the Measure of Black Men in America* (New York: Doubleday, 2005), 148.

bodies and fluids presupposes a release and exchange of a lifetime of emotions, thoughts, ideologies, preferences, and prejudices. To put it in other terms I'll express this idea as follows: when men and women masturbate or have sex with other people, we cannot, no matter how hard we try, divorce our pasts or our culture from the sex act. Even as an adolescent happily jerking off in front of the very first porn movie I ever saw, I knew *Let Me Tell Ya 'Bout White Chicks* was playing into dangerous and harmful stereotypes concerning black men and white women. Yet it surged a lust within me that still resonates even as I approach middle age. Yes, when many people have sex they like to feel that they are transgressing; nothing feels as deliciously gratifying as being a naughty boy or girl. Yet after I had satisfied my teenage lust with *Let Me Tell Ya 'Bout White Chicks*, wiped semen from my thigh with a pair of dirty boxer shorts and turned my attention to another activity, the guilt I felt over buying into the Mandingo stereotype, albeit solely, briefly and within the private confines of my own bedroom, made me question my feelings toward myself and my race. I felt I was somehow a traitor, a young African American man who hated his race and believed everything the white race had ever said about black people. The more I indulged in black man-white woman fantasies, no matter how sophisticated they were, the more my feelings of self-hatred and disgust intensified. I had to undergo a great deal of personal and sexual exploration before I could eradicate these negative feelings.

Over the years I have come to value pornography and my sexuality in all their diverse, complex, messy, and transgressive iterations. I firmly believe that whatever fantasy satiates a man's lust during the ten minutes he spends masturbating when he arrives home after a long commute, or whatever thoughts and fantasies engorge a woman's clitoris when she and her wife take time away from their rambunctious toddlers for a few minutes of passionate sex, is personal and should be enjoyed without guilt, shame, or embarrassment. Those of us who are sex positive would agree that every fantasy is permissible so long as it remains a fantasy. It should not be judged. I also believe that if we lived in a world where individuals could freely express their sexual desires without

What Color Is Your Hoodie?

fear of condemnation, punishment, ostracization or, in extreme circumstances, death, the world would be a much better place. I find it both perplexing and maddening that in the twenty-first century sexual relationships between black men and white women remain taboo. But when the partners in an interracial sexual encounter are a black man and a white man, the act becomes more aberrant than even the most open minded person can accept.

Most black gay men, after they accept their homosexuality, must inevitably answer an important question for themselves: Will I have sex with white men? I know many black gay men who, for a variety of reasons, have elected to have sex only with men of their own race and ethnicity. These reasons vary and are tangled among cultural, aesthetic, and political tethers. Those of us who seek interracial emotional and sexual relationships do so with the caveat that we may suffer worse judgments than our brothers who opt for intraracial partnerships. Although it is a cliché it holds true—the heart wants what it wants. For white gay men this is also true. As a black man married to a white man for the last sixteen years, I can say with complete certainty that my husband and I would love each other just as much if we were an intraracial couple. Yet through the years we have both had to confront narrow-minded gay men who insist our marriage is based on fetishization and not mutual love and respect. Indeed, a small number of gay men cannot even comprehend the idea that two men can actually feel more than short-term animalistic lust for one another. For them, racist stereotypes are the only authentic aspect of interracial sex.

Pornography, the arena where sex, commerce, sexuality, politics, and history frolic, both illuminates and complicates human sexuality. Most men do not take time to deconstruct their pornographic inclinations, and those of us who do risk a great deal in exposing our proclivities. Candid discussions of sex puts marriages, careers, relationships, reputations, and self-perceptions at stake, yet engaging in such conversations is crucial in obtaining a better understanding of human sexuality. We are at our most human when we are sexual. As a character on one of my favorite television shows, *Six Feet Under*, once said, "Real fucking overthrows governments."

Every social movement implicitly touts the truism that the personal is, indeed, political. Sex is a political act in which the mind and body either conform to political systems or rebels against them.

Anyone horny enough or curious enough to peruse the selections on Nakedsword, Myvidster, Xtube, and other websites which offer pornographic videos of men of all races and ethnicities having sex with other men will notice a sizable demand for big black dicks. They are sucked, they are fucked, and they are worshipped. The big black dick, as massive, sleek and injurious as a truncheon, is the Holy Grail for many sexually active gay men. While straight porn stars and filmmakers have gone out their way to exploit and perpetuate the stereotype that African American men possess extraordinarily large penises (as mentioned before, one black man working in straight porn has capitalized on his prodigious fourteen inch penis by calling himself Mandingo, thereby demonstrating his willingness to embrace the stereotype and allow the adult industry to exploit him in that way) those men who produce and participate in gay porn have been more subversive in their promulgation of the Mandingo stereotype.

Despite the demand for black penises in porn, black men themselves, as inferred from Marc Dylan's quasi-confession, are *personae non-gratae* in the mainstream of contemporary gay life, a discriminatory practice that finds harsh and unapologetic expression in gay pornography. Even among gay men, a group that has experienced as much hatred, violence, and marginalization as African Americans, white supremacy is still practiced and upheld through disaggregation of the black male body. The men who inhabit the core of gay culture—bourgeois metropolitan white men—may desire our cocks, asses, chests, biceps, and other parts, yet a wholly integrated black man with a heart, mind, and soul, a black man who is intellectual, self-supporting, articulate, and culturally and politically engaged, seldom gains entry into their elite circle. Cornell West writes, "interracial sex and marriage is the most perceived source of white fear of black people—just as the repeated castrations of lynched black men cries out for serious psychocultural explanation"[4] Interracial same-sex sex belies the racism inflected in the gay community and forces all gay men to confront the origins of their sexual desires and biases honestly. Yet racism also manifests in the fetishization of the other, a practice that occurs among gay men of all races and ethnicities.

As a veteran performer and one of the most recognizable black gay porn stars of the last decade, Diesel Washington, depending on one's perspective, is either the right person to lambaste the gay porn industry's blatant racism or, at worst, a catty hypocrite. Pornography adheres to no prescribed standards save for those imposed by communities. Studios enjoy the liberty of artistic expression when producing pornographic films, and like all cinema adult movies combine both art and commerce. Yet unlike mainstream films, porn flicks, I argue, are much more consumer driven. Porn stars like Diesel Washington can use the medium to revise the racist images inflected within adult entertainment. Gay erotica and its participants, black and white alike, have the power to challenge consumers' biases and prejudices by providing a counternarrative to white supremacist depictions of black men within Western cultural consciousness but they must be willing to do so. Regardless, the only sure way to eliminate racism in gay porn is to eradicate it from the LGBT community, which is to say Western culture must undertake the monumental project of dismantling its racist structure.

Three

As a small boy I hated to get my hair combed. Sitting cross-legged on the floor, my head bobbed between my mother's thighs as she slathered Royal Crown Hair Grease onto my scalp and dragged a comb through my tangled naps, her determination akin to a farmer desperately plowing dryland. No matter how hard I gnashed my teeth or shouted, she labored to transform my hair and make me look presentable. James Baldwin, in voice over, recounts the same experiences in a short non-narrative film titled *My Childhood*, of his mother's constant efforts to mold him into an acceptable standard of

---

4. Cornell West. *Race Matters*. (Boston: Beacon Press, 2001), 86-87.

white beauty by combing the kinks out of his hair and rubbing gobs of lotion into his ashy skin. Yet for all these ministrations Baldwin was still subject to verbal abuse from his stepfather who regularly referred to him as "frog eyes".

    I envied white boys when I was a youth because their hair was soft and straight, and I didn't think they had to go through a painful process to look good. Some were blond, some brunette, some ginger, yet all the black boys had wooly black hair that had been greased, combed and picked into submission, or shaved off altogether. I had watched enough television to know that white boys, just like white girls, possessed a quality of attractiveness that seemed to set them on a higher plane than everyone else. Their parents dressed them in stylish clothes, and even when the boys traded their slicked-back hair and pressed trousers for Mohawks and grungy denim during adolescence their parents and peers acknowledged and praised their handsomeness. Alex P. Keyton (*Family Ties*), Ricky Stratton (*Silver Spoons*), Bubba Higgins (*Mama's Family*), and Doogie Howser (*Doogie Howser, MD*) were among the many good looking white boys I regularly watched on television and envied. Their elevated economic status aside, these boys had the ability to captivate audiences and legions of teenage girls and boys (Allan Kayser who played Thelma Harper's virile redneck grandson Bubba on *Mama's Family* inspired more than a few of my adolescent wet dreams) with their pretty faces, shiny hair, and iridescent smiles. Most of the white boys I attended primary and secondary school with came from families not much higher on the socioeconomic ladder than my own, yet I and the other black boys in my environment had been inculcated to believe these white boys would go farther in life than we would, regardless of their grades and other achievements, unlike us whose skin made us public enemies. Their beauty never had to conform to the culture. It was the culture.

    I have always disliked the term "all American" in reference to beauty because the phrase applies to strikingly handsome white men with sunny blond hair, cerulean eyes, alabaster skin, and tall, athletic physiques, men who possess the Apollonian beauty so often pictured in advertisements for Ralph Lauren and Abercrombie and Fitch.

What Color Is Your Hoodie?

Even the black models in these ads—of all shades and body types—exhibit a masculine pulchritude that appeals primarily to a white gaze, a beauty that simultaneously allures yet is nonthreatening, is handsome without being overtly sexual, placates consumers who demand racial and ethnic diversity in advertising yet succeeds only in promoting tokenism. "All American" is a restrictive appellation, one that, by construction, deems any man who does not fit into such a narrow range of beauty un-American. Men of color, African American men specifically, routinely fall prey to the charge of un-American-ness (anyone who has followed to rise of Barack Obama from community organizer to president of the United States should be well aware of this). Our appearance has subjected black men to a vile aggregation of injustices. Ironically, as the nation's demography becomes browner and less Eurocentric, the cultural concept of an "all American" look should and must change. The construction of male beauty, just as female beauty, is primed for urgent redefinition.

The corresponding issue connecting gay men's penchant for bodybuilding and our engagement with pornography is beauty. Most men regardless of race, class, or sexual orientation are reluctant to admit their longing to be beautiful and desirable, heterosexual men in particular. Long thought of as the exclusive province of women, beauty has become a topic of interest for both sexes in the twenty-first century as shifts in gender and sexual identity have dislodged such discussions from their segregated cultural environs. Metrosexuals (and appearance-conscious straight men reluctant to embrace that label) owe a large debt to gay men for exporting beauty from our community into theirs. Yet the ugly truth is that within the gay community beauty belongs to white men; men of color are only privileged with beauty insofar as our appearance mimic's that of white men. Both racism and colorism thrive within the gay community, with light-skinned and white-skinned black men granted freedom to move beyond Western culture's racist proscriptions while their brown-skinned and dark-skinned brothers remain captive to fetishization and segregation.

His name was Clyde Southridge. From the time I entered junior high school until the day I graduated high school he was the most popular boy in my class, winning the esteem of both his peers and adults. Clyde carried within him the perfect combination of brains, athleticism, wit, and charisma. To my knowledge he had no enemies. No one had a bad word to say against him, which is one of the reasons I disliked him so much. In our predominantly black high school Clyde stood out for various reasons. His family, though they weren't wealthy, lived a comfortable life compared to the rest of us. His mother taught at another school in the area and many of our faculty members knew her socially or by reputation. He had an older brother, Rex, who was a senior the year we began high school. Clyde inherited the massive popularity his big brother enjoyed and as a freshman found himself the equal of upperclassmen while the rest of the freshman boys had to endure torments and beat downs. Girls swooned over both Clyde and Rex; neither ever found himself without a girlfriend. In the social hierarchy they were superstars and retained that status throughout high school. As the two smartest black boys in our class, Clyde and I had developed a friendly rivalry. We didn't occupy the same social circle (he was much too cool; I was very much a nerd) but we remained cordial to one another face to face while talking smack about each other to our friends. We belonged to the same clubs and had friends in common, yet a friendship between us never developed. To this day I wonder if the main reason Clyde and Rex enjoyed so much popularity was that they were both so utterly beautiful to behold. Being biracial, they had tawny skin, light green eyes, and sandy hair that became curly if it were left uncut. They possessed the thin pointy noses of East coast aristocrats and a haughty carriage as they swaggered up and down the halls of our school with cool self-assurance. Of course other biracial students attended our high school, but Clyde and Rex inhabited a rarified sphere all their own. They both identified as black and aligned themselves with all aspects African American culture. Yet in regard to phenotype, one had to search their faces carefully to recognize their African features. So much of their appearance could be classified as Caucasian that were it not for the hue of their skin one would hardly guess they had a black father.

What Color Is Your Hoodie?

The resentment I felt toward Clyde, then as it does now, made me feel very ashamed of myself. As an adult I concede that I undeservedly projected a host of my own anxieties over being unpopular onto Clyde. I have no way of knowing what fears, doubts, or troubles may have plagued Clyde or his brother, yet from what I observed they had little to burden them. Memories of adolescence usually commix angst, fantasy, and embellishment, making it difficult to discern fact from fiction. Yet the feelings I experienced remain as true today as they were when I experienced them all those years ago. I hold no bias against biracial individuals; as interracial relationships become more and more prominent in the United States, and as people of color advance politically, socially, and economically, it seems that although we are not in a post-racial era (I seriously doubt we ever will be) the United States is gradually entering an era where racial identity is up for grabs, and that biracial individuals like Clyde and Rex can finally choose their racial category. In short, if they want to trounce the one drop rule and choose to live their lives as Caucasians they can. I take umbrage, however, with biracial individuals who try to have it both ways, those who decry white privilege while still benefiting from it, those who proclaim their African American heritage when it wins them admiration in certain circles yet pass for white when doing so reaps rewards. Such hypocrisy is a hostile point of contention for African Americans.

The GET BIGGER! poster I crafted and hung on my bedroom wall years ago was an attempt to transform myself in myriad ways. To get bigger is to take up space in the world, to be seen after years spent cloaked in invisibility. I wanted to enlarge all aspects of my life, to extend beyond my sheltered existence, my shyness and lack of self-confidence and become larger than my environment, to bust through my own limitations. I was able to accomplish this not only through bodybuilding but also through writing, an art that forces the writer to enlarge his or her sensibilities, to engorge the linguistic might of the world, and in turn flex his own writer's muscle. Beauty, too, is an artistic project, a craft of aesthetic possibilities, a form of resistance, and a winding path toward salvation. Transforming the human body through diet and exercise is an endeavor which requires discipline, tolerance, sacrifice, and inexhaustible patience. Few have it; fewer can acquire it. Consider the bodybuilder's tools: diet and weights, his eye for symmetry and proportion, his regal bearing, posture, and stride. Consider the fullness of his muscles, their sweep and sinews, their striation. Consider too the beauty alive within in him: the millions of microscopic histories, the potential to alter, shape and reshape, to replicate energy which spins life into art and spins art into the divine. The body of a well-made man is indeed a most exquisite work of art.

Blackness, for so long, has been viewed as the absence of beauty and the epitome of evil. Defined against whiteness (itself a constructed identity), blackness subsumes the ugliness of a culture desperate for a repository to discard its own shame, ignorance, malcontent, and abuses. This has been the inglorious burden of all black people. While black women publicly vocalize and campaign against racist patriarchal renderings and negation of their beauty, this issue has been the private struggle of modern black men, full of the conundrums and contradictions fraught within our culture. In many ways black men have become, as writer Ellise Cose has determined, the envy of the world. To the dominant culture we are exotic and we are sexy, we are sexualized and we are objectified, but are we beautiful? We make the music people want to dance to but do they hear us when we cry for help? We profit the sports industry billions of dollars each year but does anyone care if the running back is only semi-literate or if the point guard is suffering from post-traumatic stress? We are paragons of masculinity but does anyone come to our aid when we are vulnerable and afraid? We are the most fascinating subject for sociologists and ethnographers yet do they ever try to rescue us from the violence and racism which keep so many of us locked in cycles of addiction, abuse, and incarceration? So long as black men remain imprisoned between the world's envy and its scorn we will never be more than an amalgam of all it fears and despises, all that is loathsome and ugly. To be beautiful, after all, is to be truly seen.

Bibliography

hooks, bell. *We Real Cool: Black Men and Masculinity*. New York: Ramparts, 2004.

McBride, Dwight A. *Why I Hate Abercrombie and Fitch: Essays on Race and Sexuality*. New York: New York University Press, 2005.

Poulson-Bryant, Scott. *Hung: A Meditation on the Measure of Black Men in America*. New York: Doubleday, 2005.

West, Cornell. *Race Matters*. Boston: Beacon Press, 2001.

Let's Talk About Interracial Porn

Historical and cultural tensions surrounding issues of masculinity, race, violence, sexuality, and miscegenation commix in both all-black and interracial pornography. Black men in gay porn customarily inhabit a position of power that has roots in racialized fetishism. To be blunt, black gay porn stars, when they are engaged in sex with white, Latino, or Asian costars, almost always perform as "tops," the penetrative partner. Anatomically, these men possess athletic physiques, very dark skin, and penises that are much longer than the average five to seven inches most men's penises measure when erect. Dwight McBride states:

> In the all-black genre and in the blatino genre, black men are represented as "trade": men with hard bodies and hard personalities to match them, men from or tied to ghetto or street life in one way or another, men possessing exceptionally large penises ... and, more often than not, men as sexual predators or aggressors.

Bobby Blake was a veteran black performer who, over the years, unleashed unbridled ultra-masculine dominance over the many white men he had sex with on camera. A towering man with a solid herculean physique, inky dark skin, plump lips, and a broad nose, Blake was never anally penetrated on camera. Blake maintained a long, successful career in gay porn and cultivated an avid fan base, but in 2000 he retired from the industry to become a minister. His stern, menacing appearance contrasts with those of black men who work in straight porn who must "be nonthreatening enough to appeal to ... white men who [want] to jerk off to images of little virginal white girls being deflowered" (Poulson-Bryant). The black men hired to work in gay porn appear to be chosen for the opposite reason: the more threatening they appear and the larger their penises, the more popularity they garner.

Bobby Blake was no exception. His final film, *Niggas' Revenge*, boldly transgresses virtually every social, political, and sexual taboo in Western culture. Blake, along with two other African American co-stars, exacts revenge on a small group of backwoods white racists by imprisoning, torturing, and sodomizing them. The actors in this film inhabit their roles convincingly, shouting racial epithets and embodying the worst stereotypes of both African-American and Caucasian men. The marriage of extreme cruelty and outré sex in *Niggas' Revenge*, which includes BD/SM, fisting, urolangia, and biastophilia, rather than making me feel uncomfortable, tantalized me. Sex aside, language is much more provocative than most sex acts and has the potential to cause more damage to an individual. Not only does *Niggas' Revenge* confirm the deep seeded beliefs of closet racists, it "referenc[es] the ugly historical and ideological realities out of which [black and gay sexual identities] have been formed" (Reid-Pharr). The verbal assaults in *Niggas' Revenge*— even the title, which supposes a white racist gaze—is far more incendiary and repugnant than the debauchery that takes place on screen. Unlike the all-black genre of gay pornography, interracial gay pornography has the potential to provoke hostile encounters among its participants simply because it stubbornly relies on a white patriarchal rendering of black male sexuality and the full inventory of racist stereotypes ascribed to black men to fuel the lust of participants and viewers alike.

The catalogue of black gay porn, in which all of the participants are of African descent, ascribes to conventions that are common in gay porn: straight male seduction, muscle worship, and exhibitionism can all be found in gay porn specifically marketed to a black viewership. Yet leather, bear, and fetish porn for black men is nonexistent: these films make no distinction between races. Any black men who perform in these films do so alongside men of other races and ethnicities. Moreover, black gay porn includes scenarios that are not found in porn for Caucasian, Latino, or Asian

What Color Is Your Hoodie?

gays. In all-black films issues of class—the street thug conquering the middle-class black male, for example—and economic and social stratifications abound. The thug, outfitted in baggy jeans, an oversized white T-shirt and Timberland boots, has become the twenty-first century's symbol of reckless and raw masculine sexual energy. As such, he appeals to many gay men regardless of their race, economic or social status. He is viewed as rebellion incarnate, a repository of the culture's racial tensions and sexual repression.

Some young black gay men, motivated by a desire to distance themselves from the rampant homophobia that exists within the African-American community, have adopted the homo-thug façade as a means of declaring their masculinity while simultaneously embracing their desire for same-sex sex. Yet these men are loath to classify themselves as gay or bisexual. As a result, some engage in "down low" behavior. According to Keith Boykin, "the hypermasculinity of hip hop culture ... created the homo-thug and the down low." The glorification of criminality, misogyny, and homophobia endorsed by hip hop artists through not only their lyrics but their lifestyle as well serves as the standard by which a sizable population of young black men gauges their masculinity. The homo-thug embodies qualities that make him a social and sexual outlaw. He has the ability to cross sexual boundaries and maintain his masculinity by dint of his racial classification and his ability to perform an unimpeachable version of masculinity, possessing "a fantastic insatiable animal sexuality that will fuck you tirelessly and still be ready for more" (McBride).

The homo-thug presents white-collar gay white men with an opportunity to indulge their lust without leaving the insular world they inhabit. By viewing interracial gay porn, gay white men who purposely distance themselves from genuine relationships with African-American men can indulge their private sexual fantasies while allowing racist and stereotypical beliefs regarding black men to persist. As bell hooks observes, "Euro-Americans seeking to leave behind a history of their brutal torture, rape, and enslavement of black bodies [project] all their fears onto black bodies." Even middle- and upper-class African American gay men long to be sexually dominated by the homo-thug, who functions as a catalyst for their reclamation of an essential notion of blackness they may feel they have tossed aside. The fetishization of the black male body, hence the black penis, emblemizes hypersexuality and masculine dominance while reinforcing the racist notion of white supremacy.

Gay pornography is considered a specialty market in the adult entertainment industry. Naturally, it appeals to a much smaller segment of the population, yet within this subdivision of the industry exists a multitude of studios that provide a sexual outlet for the desires of gay and bisexual men. The major studios film in scenic locations and employ only the most handsome and physically fit models. Each studio caters to the specific tastes of gay and bisexual men on the basis of fetish (e.g. leather, BD/SM, barebacking) or a particular type of model. Falcon Studios primarily showcases white men, either boyish and ectomorphic or athletic and in their prime, between the ages of eighteen and thirty-five. Colt Studios specializes in films starring steroid-pumped bodybuilders over thirty years old. Titan Media, perhaps the most sophisticated of the studios, regularly casts burly men over thirty. The cadre of men under contract with Titan Media crosses racial, ethnic, and international lines, though Caucasian men make up the largest section of Titan models. The cast of men who perform in Titan Media films range from beefy, hairy DILFs to heavily tattooed counterculture punks to preppie clean-shaven men who represent what is commonly called the "all-American" look. Since 1995, Titan Media has been highly successful in luring viewers into a fantasy world populated by rugged, stunningly handsome men with overdeveloped physiques who fuck each other wildly in implausible scenarios.

At the beginning of the millennium, Titan Media introduced a new star to its films. His demeanor and his aggressive sexual performance set him apart from other Titan Media stars and other black performers in general. Dred Scott is unlike any other man in gay porn. Of indeterminate origins—virtually no information can be obtained regarding his private life—Dred Scott's looks and temperament inspire as much fear as they do lust. Scott first appeared in the Titan Media film *Fallen Angel IV: Sea Men* in 2003.

What Color Is Your Hoodie?

The star of the film, inspired by Jean Genet's seminal gay novel *Querelle of Brest*, Scott plays a seaman roaming a docked freighter dressed only in dark pants, suspenders, work boots, and a black beanie as he engages in a variety of sex acts with fellow seaman. Part of Titan's fetish collection, *Fallen Angel IV: Sea Man* showcases Scott as he exhibits his penchant for aggressive sex, violent thrusting, slapping, and rough language, elements that would later become Dred Scott's trademark. In the Titan Media feature *Trespass*, Scott plays an escaped convict on the lam from several groups of bounty hunters (all of them white) who seek to recapture him. He scrambles through the wilderness shackled and handcuffed, dressed in a blue prisoner's uniform in search of new clothes and a tool to cut his bonds. Once he finds bolt cutters and new clothes, free at last, he has his way with a brawny bounty hunter (Patrick Knight) in the bed of the latter's pickup truck. *Slammer*, a film that takes places in prison, opens with Scott, acting as the prison warden, subjecting a wiry new inmate, Billy Wild, to violent sex and verbal abuse while a guard watches, aroused.

No single aspect of Dred Scott's persona can sufficiently capture what distinguishes him from his African-American peers. Perhaps the one thing that makes him different is that he has never been marketed as a black performer. Titan Media's other major black performers of the 2000s, Ben Jakks and Diesel Washington, had no choice but to be marketed in a way that confined them to essential and often stereotypical characterizations of black masculinity, and both appeared only in interracial films. In almost all of their films they were the only black males who star in the film, and they never shared sex scenes with other black performers. Ben Jakks, who is British, has unblemished bronze skin, no tattoos, a bald head, and a basketball player's sleek physique. In his five Titan films, he was often cast as a mysterious seducer. His sex scenes are imbued with a sensuousness that most pornographic films lack, and his approach to his co-stars—typically boyish white men—is tender and nonthreatening. Diesel Washington, for a time the reigning black performer for Titan, is an avatar of the ferocious black stud realized by Bobby Blake. His name—a combination of the surnames of actors Vin Diesel and Denzel Washington—trumpets his embrace of these two performers, one an action film star of multiracial extraction and the other a critically acclaimed black actor working in mainstream cinema. Diesel Washington made ten movies for Titan since he began working for the studio in the mid-00s. In his films he performs as a strict top. Like Ben Jakks, Diesel Washington is tall and lithe, yet in contrast to Jakks' seductive image, Washington's persona, buttressed by his heavily tattooed dark skin and sexual prowess, bears more relation to the homo-thug. While Jakks presents a version of black masculinity that is genteel and rather cosmopolitan, Washington fully embraces the stereotype of the menacing, hostile black man located squarely in the ghetto fantasies of Titan's largely gay white audience.

Completing the trio of top black performers exclusively contracted with Titan Media during this period is the enigmatic Dred Scott. Though not seductive like Ben Jakks or as easily categorized as a homo-thug like Diesel Washington, Dred Scott, given his obvious multiracial background—the word "Black" is tattooed on his right pectoral, and the word "White" is tattooed on his left, both in Old English type—was allowed more access into the erotic fantasy world of Titan Media. Dred Scott's stage name evokes the United States' original sin of slavery, mixing his viewers' erotic imagination with the destructive legacy of racism. However we may object to this rational or protest against it "race is a salient variable in the sex-object choices we make in the gay marketplace of desire … [and] those who benefit unduly under such a system (whites) have a great deal invested in depoliticizing desire" (McBride). Given his racial blend, the fury contained in his facial expressions, his manic thrusting during sexual intercourse, and his penchant for sadomasochism, one can easily imagine Scott as a vengeful mulatto conceived during the rape of a slave woman by her white master.

The real Dred Scott was born a slave in Virginia approximately two decades after the founding of the United States. He is famous for having unsuccessfully sued his master for his freedom, in a Supreme Court case now known as the *Dred Scott Decision*, which held that his bondage to his master remained in force even

What Color Is Your Hoodie?

in territories where slavery was illegal. Under the weight of such massive historical, racial, cultural, and sexual systems, it is impossible not to draw a number of conclusions regarding gay porn star Dred Scott's function within the sphere of erotic entertainment, and the messages, whether intentional or not, he wishes viewers to glean from his work. Notwithstanding the various motives that might come into play, including financial ones—it has been suggested that Dred Scott was a heterosexual man who did gay porn because it paid better than straight—it seems unlikely that he would adopt the name of one of the nation's most heroic African-American men without being aware of it implications. If our sexual desires are in essence a manifestation of our hidden needs and fears, they can also subsume our hatred and disgust. By reincarnating Dred Scott the slave, Dred Scott the porn star was communicating to viewers that our erotic ideation cannot be divorced from historical, political, and cultural realities.

"Because of the legacy of white supremacy and its persistence in the form of white American racism, the notions we have evolved of what stands as beautiful and desirable are thoroughly racialized," wrote Dwight A. McBride (2005). McBride also writer, "our ideas about aesthetics in the broadest sense are shot through with racial considerations that render attempts at depoliticizing them impossible." Unlike his forebear Bobby Blake or his colleagues Ben Jakks and Diesel Washington, Dred Scott's appearance—skin the color of butter pecan ice cream, an aquiline nose, rippling muscles, a stubble-shaved head, reddish-brown facial hair, and a torso clad in black tattoos that resemble armor—is more closely aligned with notions of white male beauty. This affords him the opportunity to traverse realms of sexual exchange in areas of gay erotica into which few men of color are allowed to venture. In essence, Scott's light skin serves as currency even more than his penis or ferocious sexual energy. Although Scott's African-American ancestry is unquestionable, it is equally clear that he has Caucasian genes. Similar to house slaves in the antebellum South, Scott is white enough for his white costars, producers, and directors to grant him entry into a rarefied space among the elite of gay porn, yet still black enough to keep him at a distance from his fans, white and black alike, as an archetype of the homo-thug.

Despite this license to enhance his homo-thug image, Dred Scott is still bound to the narrowly defined roles assigned to black men in gay porn. He performs on camera as an exclusive top, often exhibiting a domineering, hypermasculine persona. In the seven Titan Media films he starred in, he subjected his submissive white and Latino partners to verbal abuse, slapping, spitting, body slamming, and urination. These acts are not uncommon in mainstream gay porn: sexual acts that were once confined to specialty or fetish films have gradually encroached into more popular productions. At some point in their careers, porn actors of all races and ethnicities participate in aberrant forms of sexual expression on camera. Bobby Blake in *Niggas' Revenge* displayed behaviors far more sadistic than any that Dred Scott engaged in on camera, yet his character in *Niggas' Revenge* operates within a system of sexual debauchery alive with racist and homophobic extremism. The entire film glories in depravity.

The sadomasochism that Dred Scott enacts upon his costars appears to come from an ambiguous place of rage, once again owing to his resistance to racial and ethnic classification. When Bobby Blake abuses white men in *Niggas' Revenge*, viewers know without a doubt that the "rage" he expresses, as the title promises, is racial at root. Dred Scott is often cast as an anonymous drifter in his films. He speaks very little dialogue and, in keeping with the element of fantasy in these films, he embarks on sexual odysseys in which he alone determines the narrative course of action and which sex acts will be performed. Yet his sexual prowess and dominance do not obviate his limited function within gay porn. Despite Dred Scott's ability to alter and expand the homo-thug archetype, he is still bound to its strictures: he is never the object of seduction in these scenarios, and he is never sexually passive with white men.

The sexual dominance exercised over white men speaks volumes about Dred Scott's body as a site where historical, racial, and masculine systems converge. And yet, like all African-American men engaged in gay pornography, he is confined to a role that forces

What Color Is Your Hoodie?

black men to avoid expressing any authentic homosexual desire. McBride continues: "The ideological lessons taught and propagated by [such] films are that white men have sex with black men for reasons having to do with master fantasies and power, retributive sex ... or to trade on their value as currency in the gay marketplace of desire." Black men bottoming for white men on camera remains a taboo in films produced by major gay adult studios such as Titan.

Western culture's insistence on preserving the Mandingo myth, and its propagation in films, television programs, advertisements, and homophobic hip hop lyrics, makes it difficult for men in the gay marketplace of desire to feel comfortable with the idea of black men, especially hypermasculine black men like Dred Scott, sexually submitting to white men. To some extent this discomfort stems from the belief that white men topping black men is somehow inherently racist, an idea that harks back to the same tensions surrounding pornographic scenarios involving white men and black women. But this argument has more to do with power than race. In his incendiary, vituperative, and fiercely homophobic rants in *Soul on Ice*, Eldridge Cleaver lambastes black gay homosexuals, claiming that we have a racial death-wish as expressed in the act of being sexually submissive with white men. Since white men, by and large, hold political and economic power in Western culture, in the realm of erotic desire a reversal of roles, where black men hold dominance and white men must submit to them, balances the power differential. Yet as African American men gain political and economic power (as evidenced chiefly by the election of Barack Obama as the nation's first black president) the dynamics which have traditionally ordered gay erotica and pornography are slowly evolving.

While the major studios continue to resist sexually subordinating black men to white men, smaller and emerging studios are producing some interracial gay porn in which black men bottom for white men. Planta Rosa Productions, which specializes in gonzo bareback films (unscripted films which involve unprotected anal sex), features black men—primarily Brazilian and Afro-Caribbean—who perpetuate the Mandingo stereotype, but it balances these scenes with others in which black men are topped by white ones. In all of these scenarios, the white top is a performer who goes by the mononym Igor. Well-endowed, lanky, and hairy, with dark circles beneath his eyes, Igor mugs for the camera whenever he performs, contorting his face in a variety of goofy expressions as he thrusts and ruts inside of his costars, black and white alike, with gleeful abandon. White porn star and director Marco Paris performs almost exclusively with black men, though he assumes both active and passive roles. What is interesting about this inversion of the norm is that the tops in these cases are not American: Igor is Russian and Marco Paris is Slovakian. The fact that only European white men are allowed to sexually dominate men of African descent highlights the insidiousness of racism that pervades American society and the comfort black men feel sexually submitting to white men who are not descended from slave owning ancestors.

The black male body historically has served both as a repository of Western culture's most ardent and prurient desires, and its hatred and disgust of racial and sexual "others." Dred Scott's career in gay pornography ended as quickly and mysteriously as it began. After making seven films with Titan Media, he had no further public engagement with erotic entertainment. Dred Scott may have freed himself from the need to do gay porn, but his persona on camera remains captive to the social systems that perpetuate racist and homophobic myths and stereotypes regarding African-American men and gay men. The paradox of acquiring fame within the gay adult entertainment industry is no more or less problematic for Dred Scott than it is for all men of color. In an era when those who inhabit the ultraconservative fringe continue to lob racist attacks at President Obama, the de facto symbol of black masculinity in the twenty-first century, even as the gay rights movement is gaining greater support among Americans, I find it damning that our culture is still unwilling to relinquish its addiction to destructive, shameful, and anachronistic representations of black gay sexuality. Perhaps Dred Scott felt the same way and refused to contribute to it any longer. Of course the answer may never be known. And as the social and sexual paradigms that once ordered gay pornography rapidly change, as the major studios alter their films to keep pace with not only with web-based production companies such as Tim Tales and Men at Play but also swift cultural changes within the gay community, redefinitions and realignments of all sorts will be necessary.

Works Cited

Boykin, Keith. *Beyond the Down Low: Sex, Lies, and Denial in Black America.* New York: Carroll & Graff, 2005. Print.

Cleaver, Eldridge. *Soul on Ice.* New York: Ramparts, 1968. Print.

hooks, bell. *We Real Cool: Black Men and Masculinity.* New York: Routledge, 2004. Print.

McBride, Dwight A. *Why I Hate Abercrombie & Fitch: Essays on Race and Sexuality.* New York: New York University Press, 2005. Print.

Poulson-Bryant, Scott. *Hung: A Meditation on the Measure of Black Men in America.* New York: Doubleday, 2005. Print.

Reid-Pharr, Robert F. *Black Gay Man: Essays.* New York: New York University Press, 2001. Print.

My Last Love Affair

I first heard about him in a class I took in grad school called Steal This Poem, a poetry workshop that included me—a muscular black man—and six white girls. One afternoon we were engaged in a loose conversation about all things Chicago (e.g. the Brown Line versus the Blue Line, Wicker Park hipsters, the Bucket Boys, the crazy preacher in front of Old Navy on State Street) when one of them gazed dreamily into the air and, in a lilting voice, said, "You know, every time I hear Barack Obama speak I get all sun shiny inside." A few months after, as luck would have it, I had an opportunity to hear then senatorial candidate Obama give a stump speech at a church in Oak Park, Illinois. I recall that he was quite tall and handsome in an offbeat way. My initial impression of him was that he sounded like a lot of young black men I'd heard speak in religious services when I was a kid: impassioned, articulate, adept at turning a phrase and inflecting particular words, pausing in the right places and building up to lusty applause lines. I became an Obama supporter right then and there, secure in my belief that he would win his bid. He did. This was the same year John Kerry lost the 2004 presidential race by a thin margin and dashed the hopes of liberals and progressives all over the country that George W. Bush would be a one-term president. Almost immediately Obama's name was being floated as a potential presidential candidate for 2008. American politics had never seen a candidate like this before: savvy, eloquent, dapper, highly intelligent, accessible, somewhat geeky and enticingly erudite; a man whose meteoric political rise, at an age when pols are still considered kids in the world of politics, was without precedent; who could inspire the energies and passions of the Democratic base and even draw supporters from the other side of the aisle. Oh, and he was black.

The 2008 presidential election took place in the center of a maelstrom of personal highs and lows for me. My partner and I got married three weeks earlier and my husband's mother died of cancer three weeks later. I recall those months as a time of overwhelming upheaval for us and the country. I didn't get turned on to politics until the Bush-Gore election of 2000 when, like the rest of the nation, I was on tenterhooks waiting to hear just who won the election. What followed after the Supreme Court essentially gifted the presidency to Bush was eight years of dejection and demoralization not only for me but most of the nation, and it was pretty much a tacitly accepted belief that because of the heinous damage wrought by the Bush administration and the implosion of the American economy under Bush's presidency, whoever the Democratic nominee for president was would glide into office. And Barack Obama did, handily winning 53% of the Electoral College. Until spring of 2008 I had never invested time, money, and energy to a political campaign. The most I ever did was attend a Howard Dean rally at Navy Pier in 2004. But Barack Obama's magnetism, his self-assured persona and his brainy coolness compelled me take interest. Although I am a loyal liberal Democrat and would have voted for whomever secured the Democratic nomination, having the nation's first viable African American candidate at the top of the ticket certainly motivated me and millions of other Americans to donate our money, time, hearts, and psychic energy to the Obama-Biden campaign. For months I kept up with polls and blogs, watched MSNBC and CNN round the clock, hounded friends and family about registering to vote, and made sure they got their butts out of bed on November fourth and actually went to the polls and voted. I out-pit bulled Sarah Palin. I had to—the nation's future and the survival of the Democratic Party was at stake. History was calling and every American needed to answer. We did—Barack Obama is the nation's forty-fourth president.

Hope and change remain the hallmark of Barack Obama's governance and an appeal to the down-trodden masses of Americans who gave up believing in those in power to come rescue them from

What Color Is Your Hoodie?

the ceaseless struggle of the Great Recession: unemployment, outsourcing, off shoring, vulture economics, and what each side, left and right, consider the erosion of morality and the culture's slow march toward Fascism. Given one's politics, Barack Obama either became president at the right time or the wrong time. I think what the vast majority of Americans fail to realize about President Obama, whether they are dejected liberals, fear mongering conservatives, militant Occupy protesters or radical Tea Partiers, is that he is just a man and can only accomplish so much. No President—not FDR, Truman, Reagan, or George W. Bush—governs alone. He needs the assistance of Congress. But like bratty kids, Republicans refuse to work with the President on any legislation. Whoever you are and whatever political ideology you ascribe to (if any) you cannot deny that Republicans have gone out of their way to obstruct the political process since Barack Obama took the oath of office in January 2009. Democrats may have detested George W. Bush during his eight years as president, but they knew they were elected to serve the American people and regardless of their own personal feelings about President Bush they still tried to cooperate with him to enact legislation, for better or worse. The Republicans' shocking intransigence, their never-ending conspiracy theories ("Obama is a secret Muslim; a terrorist sympathizer; a socialist; not an American citizen"), their blatant disrespect for both the man and his office, and their efforts to besmirch his political legacy reveal them to be a party not only woefully incapable of serving the needs of the American people but also a party full of racists and lunatics, people who cannot live and function in the modern world which embraces racial and ethnic diversity, science, critical thinking, equal rights, civil liberties, immigrants and minorities of every stripe. This is a party, despite trumpeting morality, family values and Christian charity, that applauds when one of its presidential candidates suggests in a national debate that terminally ill citizens who lack adequate insurance should die quickly, has no business governing. These are the maniacs Barack Obama, rather foolishly, believed he could woo across the aisle. 2008 was a wave election for Democrats that gave them complete control of every chamber of the executive branch of government. While liberals and progressive begged and pleaded for the Democrats to take advantage of their majority to force through legislation that would benefit society, the President and members of his party—while working hard to save the American economy from the brink of utter disaster—squandered their chance to protect women's reproductive rights, overturn DOMA, pass the DREAM act, and enact a laundry list of bills that would have aided the environment and help stabilize the middle class. Still, the President succeeded in saving the auto industry, killing Osama bin Laden, and, most importantly, passing the Affordable Care Act, which Republicans derisively call Obamacare. And he is never praised, never congratulated, only disrespected, hated, reviled, and plotted against.

Why our President refuses to crow about his successes and allows the radical right to construct the narrative of his presidency without attacking them (something the Clintons are masters at) perplexes many, but think of it: black men are stereotyped as violent brutes, angry, always out to steal from and harm every white person they see. Becoming an attack dog, even though it isn't in his nature, would confirm the hideous stereotypes the right so eagerly wants to perpetuate. Barack Obama's high-minded attitude toward American politics has harmed him, and now I think he finally realizes that survival on the Hill necessitates at least a modicum of dirty play. Given the rigid divisiveness of our country's political climate, the looney intractability of Republicans, and the corrosiveness of the Citizens United decision, I've made a decision to never again fall in love with a politician. I simply cannot go through this every four years.

It's time for me to come out of the closet—I love Barack Obama. I love him as the father figure I wished for during my lonely boyhood; I love him as the older brother I wanted to guide me through the embattled terrain of adulthood; I love him as the leader I would gladly sacrifice my life for in battle. I never believed I could feel such kinship and allegiance to a political leader; I never knew love and politics could blend like honey and tea—my President, my kindred, my angle, my all, my other self.

What Color Is Your Hoodie?

Barack Obama.

Like so many others I became enamored of Obama during his first presidential bid. His story is unlike mine (he has always existed among the black elite while I'm just a few paychecks away from returning to ghetto life) but we're both black men of similar political ideologies, both educated and talented. When the conservative media concoct lies about the President, when they question his birth and his patriotism, when Congressional Republicans refuse to work with him to legislate and find solutions to the many problems that plague this nation, the pit bull in me comes out snarling and barking, ready to maul and maim. I feel they're attacking me as much as the POTUS. Think of it: if the most powerful black man on the planet can't get a sizable portion of his own citizens to respect him after he's done everything he can to cooperate with them. What makes any black man in the nation believe in racial equality and justice after witnessing the attacks on the President? Mind you, these are not attacks on his policies; these are attacks on him as a person of color. And as much as I defend him, and for all the criticism I have of his sometimes sluggish and baffling politics, I can't continue to stress myself defending him and wringing my hands over polls, attack ads and fundraising on the right. Month after month I find my nerves jangled, my disposition surly, my time and attention taken up by the latest twenty-four hour news cycle or poll or nonsense uttered by a talking head or surrogate. I have headaches, trouble sleeping, and strained eyes. During the summer I hole up in my basement in front of my flatscreen and watch MSNBC for hours, log on to Huffington Post and Politico multiple times a day. During both the 2008 and 2012 campaigns I would donate fifteen dollars to the Obama campaign in the morning and ten dollars at night, tossing funds across the Internet as if I were sprinkling grass seed. Like so many others who rabidly campaigned, canvassed and hosted fundraisers for Barack Obama in 2008, I am fatigued, weathered, and dispirited. I can no longer live in the news spin.

I believe this nation is best served by Democrats, progressives, and liberals, and I will not hesitate to champion any member of the political left who deserves it. But now that the 2012 election is history, I will never again allow myself to fall in love with a politician. It's too costly in so many ways. Anyway, politicians don't need our love; they need our service. My advice is to support your own ideology, Democrat or Republican, Green party or Libertarian party or other, and not the person elected to represent it. A man is a man, a woman is a woman and we should never fall into the trap of thinking politicians are anything more. The President is not a superhero and his opponents are not supervillians. The pendulum of politics swings constantly. Eventually a Republican will be elected to the nation's highest office again. Some Republican will take up the splintered mantle left by Bush, and one day there will be a new Democrat in office. No matter who wins, I will do the smart thing and save all of my love for my friends and family. As for politicians, as the song goes, I'm through with love; I'll never fall again.

Film Studies for Black Gay Men

One of my favorite television shows is *True Blood*. Although many characters stand out, Lafayette Reynolds, the flamboyant yet tough gay cook played by Nelsen Ellis, is a fan favorite and perhaps the most beloved of all the characters on the show. What makes Lafayette so appealing, aside from being *True Blood*'s most noble character, is that he is not afraid to be who he truly is: a black gay man living in the Deep South who makes no apologies for being either black or gay. He takes tremendous pride in his identity and will not let anyone—not even a few blood thirsty vampires—make him feel like an inferior second class citizen. Lafayette is the latest in a string of black gay characters to populate the television landscape in the last decade. Since 1998, a steady stream of network and cable television shows have included a black gay character: Carter Heywood (Michael Boatman) on *Spin City*, Keith Charles (Mathew St. Patrick) on *Six Feet Under*, Omar Little (Michael K. Williams) on *The Wire*, Will Truman's brief love interest James Hanson (Taye Diggs) on *Will & Grace* are chief among them. The Gay Rights movement has engendered a great deal of discussion regarding the lives of homosexuals, and it appears that television, the most accessible outlet for those wishing to see holistic versions of themselves represented in popular culture, has taken the lead in presenting American audiences with what are perhaps the first truly complete representations of black homosexual male identity in mass culture. Although these programs have a long way to go in terms of presenting the full spectrum of black gay experience, they should and must be lauded for including and acknowledging our experiences if only minimally.

The same recognition, sadly, cannot be given to cinema. While television programs can afford to take a risk including characters and storylines that more conservative viewers may object to, studios and filmmakers, with their dogged insistence on hefty box office grosses both domestically and abroad, simply are not as willing to suffer any backlash or financial loss if audiences do not flock to see a black gay romance or an action film in which the ass-kicking protagonist is gay. Such is the distasteful reality all queers have had to live with since the days of nickelodeons. Although black veteran actors from 1950s and 60s— particularly Sidney Poitier and Harry Belafonte—can be credited for leading black men out of the backdrop of American cinema and into the spotlight, only in the last twenty years have filmmakers and audiences alike felt comfortable enough with black masculinity on screen to embrace an expansion of the roles traditionally given to black actors. Those black actors who headline big budget films and get their names billed above the title—Denzel Washington, Will Smith, Eddie Murphy, and Jamie Foxx among the biggest box office draws—have managed, with the assistance of filmmakers and screenwriters, to demonstrate an ever-widening scope of black masculinity that black audiences can champion and white audiences won't feel threatened by. Collectively, these actors have taken on roles in which they have showcased the diversity and complexity of black men of various socioeconomic backgrounds, personal philosophies, accomplishments and failings, all of which take place in myriad eras, settings, and circumstances. Yet despite the full breadth of these varied depictions of black masculinity, only one of the aforementioned actors, Will Smith in *Six Degrees of Separation*, has played an out gay man on-screen, proof that black actors still have thresholds to cross in of terms of demonstrating a complete rendering of black masculinity in films.

Though the Gay Rights Movement has greatly advanced in the years since Stonewall, the concerns of gays and lesbians of color has by and large been shadowed by the community's larger aims, not the least of which include HIV/AIDS prevention and treatment, legalizing same-sex marriage, gay adoption and foster parenting rights, and ending discrimination in both the workplace and the

What Color Is Your Hoodie?

military. The face of gay America depicted in popular culture often assumes the phenotype of pretty white men and women with stylishly coiffed hair, radiant smiles, and twinkling blue eyes who occupy middle and upper middle class environments in large metropolitan cities such as New York or San Francisco. Despite the current proliferation of black gay men on television, the two most highly profiled gay-themed shows of the last decade, *Will & Grace* and *Queer as Folk*, failed to include a single recurrent gay character of color; *Will & Grace*'s inclusion of Taye Diggs in a toss away four-episode storyline came during the show's final season. Only when *Noah's Arc* premiered on LOGO in 2005 did black gay men finally see themselves front and center on television yet after two short seasons the sitcom was canceled. In terms of gay representation in popular culture, I've come to understand that many producers and filmmakers believe it's easier for audiences to see whitewashed examples of queer culture and accept them before the viewing public can embrace gay minorities, who they may not feel so at ease with. This skewed principle is not new: the same belief has been applied historically to all minority groups that exist within the United States. Nevertheless, the claim black gay men have to their own authentic lives is placed at risk each time we are excluded from conversations regarding the rights of all LGBTQ people, for all forms of art are, at their core, a dialogue and a debate.

As hard as I try I cannot think of more than a paucity of African American gay characters throughout the long history of American cinema. A brief yet deliciously amusing scene takes place at the beginning of the 1959 film *Odds Against Tomorrow* in which Harry Belafonte, at his most devastatingly handsome, enters an elevator and the black elevator operator, as captivated by Belafonte as any gay man would be, looks him up and down in an overtly sexual manner and smiles from ear to ear, ready to devour Belafonte. In the 1970s, actor Antonio Fargas played a gay man in two films, the unmemorable *Next Stop, Greenwich Village* and the uproarious all-black comedy *Car Wash*. In spite of the dearth of well-rounded black gay male characters on screen, homophobia against black gay men in films and on television is quite easy to locate. The *Revenge of the Nerds* franchise of the 1980s featured actor Larry B. Scott in a shameless, flamboyant performance as the only black and only gay brother of the nerds' fraternity. I watched the first *Revenge of the Nerds* movie when I was still in elementary school one Friday night at a sleepover at my aunt and uncle's house. When Scott's character Lamar Latrell flounced on-screen, lisping, switching and playing into every gay stereotype, my relatives laughed heartily, but even as a child who was unaware of his own homosexuality I was disturbed by Lamar's behavior and my family's response to it. The same is true of Eddie Murphy's gay police officer sketch in his filmed concert *Raw*. *Blind Faith*, a 1998 TV movie starting Charles S. Dutton, Courtney B. Vance, Kadeem Hardison, and Lonette McKee, depicts the deterioration of a middle class black family in the late 1950s when Dutton and McKee' teenage son Charles Jr. (Garland Whitt) is arrested for murder. Late one night in a secluded area of a public park, Charles Jr. and a friend, another black teenager, are attacked by a group of white boys. Charles Jr. is charged with strangling one of them to death, an accusation he vehemently denies. Complicating the situation further is the fact that Charles Sr. is one of the few black officers on the police force. Vance, who plays Charles Jr.'s uncle, acts as his lawyer and together with the help of a group of Civil Rights activists works round the clock to free him. Viewers who assume, as I did when I first saw *Blind Faith*, that the film's primary plot revolved around the racial injustice of the era, are surprised to learn that the reason Charles Jr. and his friend were in the park alone is that they were gay lovers who were sharing an intimate moment when the gang of white boys happened upon them and terrorized them. Upon learning this, Charles Sr. disowns his son outright and no amount of pleading from his brothers or his wife convinces him to accept Charles Jr. In the end, heartbroken and hopeless, Charles Jr. hangs himself in jail. The message here is clear: the black community has no place for black men who are gay. It would appear that the greatest sin a black man can commit, greater than even murder or abandoning one's child, is being a homosexual.

These screen portrayals embody the scurrilous, hostile, and virulent homophobia that pervades the African American

What Color Is Your Hoodie?

community, which is sanctioned by the black church and proliferated in deplorable hip hop lyrics. The black gay man's body has historically served as a repository of the entire race's hatred, anger, and self-loathing. Indeed, the loudest voices of protest against the advancement of gay rights can be heard within the African American community, and the effect of this homophobia has been devastating for all concerned. Black gays and lesbians comprise the largest population of runaway and homeless youths, and African Americans are the largest demographic impacted by HIV/AIDS. The exclusion of positive images of black gay men in American cinema is both endemic and symptomatic of the toxicity of homophobia within Western culture.

When I met my husband Gerald during the final months before he defended his dissertation in 1997, he showed me a film that helped me chart a course for how I would map my life as a black gay man. *Looking for Langston*, a black-and-white non-narrative film written and directed by British filmmaker Issac Julien in 1989, is the first film to portray black gay men in a positive light and the first to candidly examine homosexuality among men of color. Set among gay speakeasies of the 1920s, where both black and white men wear elegant tuxedos, sip champagne, languorously smoke cigarettes, dance with and seduce one another, Julien's film explores the twin demons of racism and homophobia that plague gay men of color. Using the life, work, and legacy of Harlem Renaissance poet Langston Hughes as a metaphor through which we can come to a greater understanding of the cultural, historical, and artistic forces that have encumbered black homosexuals for so long, Julien exposes audiences to a world that transcends time, space, and language, one in which the loves and lusts of black gay men are freely exchanged and exist outside of white hegemonic forces, yet is never truly separated from them. Controversial photographs by Robert Mapplethorpe depicting black men in sexually objectified poses hang throughout the speakeasy, and boyish, doe-eyed angels with sparkling wings hold large photographs of Langston Hughes and James Baldwin, the progenitors of the black gay aesthetic in literature and art.

Though emancipated, for a time, from the brutality of homophobia, the smoky, dreamlike fantasy world inhabited by the men in this film harbors a great deal of racism and colorism. Potential white loves rebuff the advances of black men. Light-skinned black men, likewise, reject the affections of their darker skinned brothers. Actor Ben Ellison, playing a character named Alex, pursues Beauty, as embodied by Matthew Baidoo. One of the most erotic images I have ever seen on screen is the sight of these two beautiful black men, muscular and lithe, sleeping naked and entwined head-to-foot after making love. While the film glories in the timeless dreamscape its handsome men inhabit, it also wrestles with race, racism, homophobia and, in the film's final moments, references the HIV/AIDS crisis. Yet none of these topics is addressed in a preachy or indignant tone. Like the vacuous beauty of the men in the film, these topics are merely referential, just tiny morsels for the audience to ponder as they connect the images before them with the poems of Hughes, Richard Bruce Nugent, and Essex Hemphill. Julien seems to have multiple aims with *Looking for Langston*. He wants viewers to form their own opinions regarding the film, as all artists do. Yet holistic representations of black gay men and their lives, representations that reject outright the ugly stereotypical characterizations that hitherto shaped the culture's image of African American homosexual men, seems to be his primary motivation for making this film. As polemical as any film can be, the only fight *Looking for Langston* really wants to take on is the fight for visibility and recognition.

Looking for Langston did for black gay men in the late 1980s what *Brokeback Mountain* did for the entire population of gay men in the mid-00s. Though much smaller in scale, viewership, and acclaim than *Brokeback Mountain*, *Looking for Langston*'s entry, albeit marginally, into the aggregation of modern cinema did not go unnoticed. Queer audiences, scholars, researchers, and filmmakers instantly seized upon the film and utilized it as a lens through which a variety of issues regarding race, gender, sexual orientation, representation, and human rights could be investigated. Considering the timing of the film's release—at the height of the AIDS crisis

What Color Is Your Hoodie?

and the Reagan administration's assault blacks, gays, immigrants, the homeless, the poor, and the disabled, and coinciding with the rise of gangsta rap which promotes a hypermasculine rendering of black masculinity rooted in a racist view of black men—*Looking for Langston* symbolizes the subaltern's revolt against the crushing hegemonic forces of white conservative capitalism. Black gay filmmaker and activist Marlon Riggs once said, "Black men loving black men is *the* revolutionary act." The frank exhibitions of erotic pursuits and conquests in *Looking for Langston* support this claim. The film can best be described as a form of *petit marronage* coolly administered from an entire population of individuals who have been, for so long, either denigrated by the filmic arts or ignored by them altogether.

Revolt against racist and homophobic hegemonic forces and resistance to demeaning representations propels Riggs' 1989 PBS documentary *Tongues Untied*. While *Tongues Untied* originates from the same place of longing and frustration as *Looking for Langston*, Riggs' presents a fiery indictment of Western culture more polemical than any other documentary on the subject of identity politics, gay politics in particular. *Tongues Untied* fashions together a series of brutal vignettes on topics as far ranging as racism, homophobia both within the black community and without, HIV/AIDS, masculinity and gender. It also celebrates black gay culture, encompassing "snapology," friendship, activism, and the beauty of black men. Sensuous in its exhibitions of rage and wrathful in its take on sex, the film (which gained the ire of Republican presidential candidate Pat Buchanan who lambasted it as pornographic art funded by the Bush administration) exhorts confrontation and activism as a means of combating systems of oppression and reclaiming personal identity. Riggs employs spoken word poetry (courtesy of Essex Hemphill), dancing and singing along with footage of protests marches in San Francisco's Gay Pride parade to support his thesis regarding the value and necessity of activism.

Upon my first viewing of *Tongues Untied* as an undergrad at Northwestern University thirteen years after it first aired on

PBS, I was emboldened by the documentary's fierce critique of Western culture and its underlying message concerning activism and self-love. Self-acceptance is without question the first step in enacting change within an oppressive system. Yet when I watched the documentary again eight years later I was taken aback by the rage presented on screen and embedded in Riggs' treatise. As groundbreaking as the film was when it premiered and as germane as it remains in multiple academic disciplines and artistic mediums, *Tongues Untied* has not held up well over time. Though attitudes toward homosexuals and people of color have progressed since the film's debut, they have nevertheless advanced in large part because of *Tongues Untied* and other scholarly and artistic works of its kind. The strident, vituperative tone of *Tongues Untied*, though absolutely appropriate and necessary given the era and ethos it documents, sharply contrasts *Looking for Langston*'s refined critique of racism and homophobia, which borders on luminal. *Tongues Untied*, in this regard, contributes to its own inability to transcend different eras, unlike *Looking for Langston*, which feels timeless. Yet the latter lacks the aggressiveness that makes the former so impactful. Together these films serve as a powerful weapon against the myriad abuses suffered by black gay men. Separately their effectiveness is limited by their own aesthetics.

Despite the passion and sincerity conveyed in non-narrative films, several years would pass before I finally had the chance to see an honest portrayal of black gay manhood in a feature film. During the 2005 Chicago Gay and Lesbian Film Festival, my husband Gerald and I were among the first audiences to see *Brother to Brother*, a film written and directed by Rodney Evans. In the film, Anthony Mackie stars as Perry, a college student in New York City kicked out of his family's home when his father discovers his homosexuality. Circumspect, jaded, and guarded, Perry is reluctant to form bonds with anyone other than his best friend Marcus (Lawrence Gillard, Jr.), a poet. In Perry, audiences, for the first time, are given a holistic, honest and sympathetic portrayal of a black gay man and watch him as he struggles with questions of racial, sexual, and artistic identity. Perry spends his time studying, reading, painting and working

What Color Is Your Hoodie?

at a homeless shelter. Although he is actively engaged in cultural discourse and debates identity politics both in the classroom and among acquaintances, Perry isolates himself out of fear of being hurt. Mackie plays him with measured reserve; he rarely smiles or shows much emotion. Marcus, who happens to be straight, is Perry's biggest champion and confidant. He encourages Perry to accept himself and continue to stand up for his right as a gay man to be heard. Perry embodies a mass of frustrations and resentments. Although his bitterness is undeniable, he reflects the bitterness of virtually all gay men of color who confront racism and homophobia each and every day. Rejected by his father, who evicted him from his family's home, reviled and attacked by the black community, Perry seeks solace in a relationship with Jim (Alex Burns), a white student at his university. Heretofore good buddies, Perry and Jim have a sexual encounter one drunken night in Perry's dorm room. It is Jim's first same-sex experience, and although he appears to regret the encounter only hours later, sneaking out of bed in a shell shocked daze and returning to his own dorm room much to Perry's palpable dejection, he eventually accepts his sexuality and pursues Perry, much to Perry's delight. Yet after their second sexual encounter, when they are lying together in post-coital bliss and Jim coos in Perry's ear, "I love your sweet black ass," Perry abandons any ideas he had of sustaining a meaningful relationship with Jim, abruptly dresses and leaves Jim's room.

When this scene occurred in the film, many members of the primarily black gay male audience who saw the film with Gerald and me groaned and scoffed their displeasure. What they objected to was not Perry's desire to go to bed with a white man but Jim's racial fetishization of Perry. Although Jim's remark was not intended to wound Perry, it validates all of Perry's assumptions concerning interracial sex and racism, twisting what should have been a loving sexual encounter into an expression of racism, marking Perry's body as a site of oppression, shame, and dehumanization. The only way to rid himself of these confines and reclaim his personhood is to terminate his relationship with Jim and embark on a discovery of his black gay heritage.

Perry's story only accounts for half of the plot of *Brother to Brother*. The other storyline follows a young Richard Bruce Nugent, author of the poem "Smoke, Lilies and Jade," as he befriends literary giants Langston Hughes, Zora Neale Hurston, and Wallace Thurman and becomes a key figure of the Harlem Renaissance. Perry meets Nugent in the homeless shelter where he works, and through his interactions with the older Nugent he comes to a greater understanding of his forbears, the black gay aesthetic, and personal pride. Nugent relates to Perry the struggles, loves, challenges and losses endured by the members of his coterie. (The inclusion of Nugent into the main action of the film must be seen merely as Evans' attempt to draw a connection between the black gay luminaries of the Harlem Renaissance, who were the progenitors of black gay aesthetics, politics, and social discourse, and the myriad conflicts faced by black gay men in modern America. In reality, Nugent died almost twenty years before the main plot of the film unfolds.) These scenes provide a stark contrast between these two black gay artists. While modern Harlem confines and intimidates Perry, the Harlem of the 1920s (shot in black and white) serves as a playground for the writers of the Harlem Renaissance. Perry's frustrations and ambivalence as a painter inhibit him in many ways, but Nugent, Hughes, Wallace, and Hurston, despite their inability to publish more than one issue of their controversial literary magazine *Fire!!*, refuse to allow the hegemonic forces, Caucasian and African American, racist and homophobic, to bring their creative pursuits to a halt. Perry remains confounded by sex with white men while Nugent and Wallace revel in sexual liaisons with them. The irony that Nugent and his contemporaries voraciously satisfy their artistic and sexual appetites in an era of tremendous social and sexual repression while Perry, in the more socially and sexually liberal twenty-first century, cannot do the same highlights the cost of genuine representation in the arts and forces the audience to consider how and why black gay men in the twenty-first century, who enjoy more freedom and acceptance than their forbears, currently find themselves struggling to reconcile their inner lives with their private lives and their private lives with society at large.

What Color Is Your Hoodie?

Not long ago I watched the film *Noah's Arc: Jumping the Broom* on DVD. Although the television series which served as the basis for the film never ranked among the most impressive situation comedies in television history, I admired it because there simply wasn't a show like it before. The concept of the show has been duplicated time and again, from *The Golden Girls* to *Designing Women* to *Sex and the City* to *Girls*: take four friends—the pragmatist (Douglas Spearman as Chance), the libertine (Christian Vincent as Ricky), the mama figure (Rodney Chester as Alex), and the artistic gadabout who embodies all three characters (Darryl Stephens in the lead role as Noah)—place them in a kaleidoscope of professional, personal, and romantic entanglements, watch the sparks fly and enjoy. This format traditionally favors female and gay audiences: individuals who typically rely on close friends to help resolve conflicts in their lives. Through their candid discussions over cheesecake or cosmos or brunch, viewers are supposed to get an earful of the thoughts, frustrations, desires, and opinions of modern women. Yet the spin *Noah's Arc* places on this formula gives viewers something they never had before: the voice of upwardly mobile, out black gay men in the twenty-first century. Although *Noah's Arc* had a small but devoted following it was cancelled after two seasons. The feature film was designed to tie up loose ends (yet some questions, specifically the fate of a minor character that may or may not have been killed in car crash in the second season's climax, remained unanswered) and give a happy ending for Noah and his on again, off again love interest, Wade. Sadly, what director Patrik Ian-Polk and cast present on screen is a series of implausible, nonsensical episodes leading up to a dream wedding between Noah and Wade in Martha's Vineyard. The critic in me wants to hate this movie for its cookie cutter characterizations, clichéd plots, and flights of melodrama, yet as a black gay man I yearn for representation, for a chance to see someone like me in a film living a life as close to my own as possible. Noah and his friends don't succeed in advancing our cinematic depictions beyond the swishy exhibitions of Lamar Latrell, yet they take us closer to verisimilitude than we have been. And every success, no matter how small, must be celebrated.

The quest for holistic representation in art has, is, and always will be arduous. For minorities, particularly sexual minorities, gaining control of our filmic representations is one way to combat the negative images the film industry flickers into the public's consciousness. But doing so requires not only capital and access to the means of production, but visionary storytellers and filmmakers. Indeed, without the vision and courage of Isaac Julien, Marlon Riggs, Rodney Evans, and Patrik Ian-Polk, the slim cannon of black gay cinema would be non-existent. Their works engendered the strides made by black gay men in the last two decades to acquire the full inventory of civil liberties, personal pride, and social equality and will continue to do so for years to come.

Teaching Black, Living Gay

For the last seven years I have been employed at Aurora University, a small private institution nestled among mid-century homes in Aurora, Illinois, a middle class suburb west of Chicago. I am the Assistant Director of the Center for Teaching and Learning. The CTL provides academic support to the entire university, primarily in the form of tutoring in writing, which is my field. Each day I go to work I sit down with students, either individually or in workshops, enrolled in courses across many different disciplines and guide them through the writing process. The majority of the students I work with are first generation college freshmen; others are middle aged graduate students primarily in the fields of social work and nursing earning an advanced degree so they can switch careers. Some seek only "a second pair of eyes" to give them constructive criticism of a writing project, while others require comprehensive tutoring in essential grammar and writing mechanics they failed to receive during their elementary and secondary education. One of the benefits of my job is that it allows me to read scholarship related to a variety of topics (in a single day I can read papers from courses in literature, sociology, nursing, social work, history and business administration) yet it also affords me the unhappy task of confronting the many ways the education system in the United States fails.

My contract at Aurora University requires me to teach one course each semester for the General Education department: Introduction to Literary Study in the fall and Culture and Diversity in the spring. Last year, with the approval of my department chair, I took an alternative approach to the course. Instead of the usual canonical readings I list on my syllabus—the litany of dead white men from Shakespeare to Hemingway and the handful of women and people of color customarily included in virtually every literature anthology—I devoted this semester's class to the works of African American writers. AU's student population is almost equally divided between African American, Caucasian, and Latino students, and a course in black literature, I believed, would be quite successful (African American Literature, as an independent course, hasn't been taught at AU in five years). I contacted a textbook distributor and inquired if he could recommend a good textbook for the class. To my great delight, he sent me a brand new copy of the second edition of *The Norton Anthology of African American Literature.* Edited by Henry Louis Gates, Jr. and Nellie Y. McKay and over two thousand seven hundred pages long, the textbook is the most comprehensive collection of writings from African Americans I've ever seen. This bulky tome contains spirituals, sermons, speeches, slave narratives, short stories, novellas, novel excerpts, poems, and plays by the United States' most noted black authors. A teacher's manual and two compact discs, one containing music (gospel, jazz, blues, R&B, and hip hop), the other speeches and spoken word poems, were included in the box the distributor sent. For me, an African American educator and writer, this textbook is a veritable treasure trove. Never before have I seen or possessed such an extensive collection of literature written by black Americans, full of the breadth of African American experience. At this particular moment in American history, with the nation's first African American president leading the nation and the apoplectic ultraconservative fringe making every attempt to delegitimize his presidency and invalidate his citizenship; with select African Americans leading Fortune 500 corporations and shattering the glass ceiling not only in politics and finance but academia, medicine and science as well; with black arts and black artists growing more eclectic with each passing year, now, I believe, is the perfect time to gather a group of eighteen-year olds, force them to turn off their beeping, chirping electronic gadgets, and engage them in a discussion not only of African American literature but also history, gender, sexuality, class, and the politics tethered to each.

What Color Is Your Hoodie?

This evening my husband asked me how I would respond if one of my students asks, "Why do I have to take this course?" The short answer is the course is a requirement for degree completion. Yet this question, despite its obvious narcissism and anti-intellectual subtext, deserves a rich response. If a student ever posed this question to me I'd be moved to ask her or him, "Why do people write?" Likely this retort would elicit little more than a shrug or eye-rolling. Writers write to make sense of the world. They seek to map the complex psychic terrain of human experience, to make sense of a world that often makes no sense. Creative writing speaks the unspoken for those who cannot or do not speak, mining the interior life of people to excavate that which is universal. A criminal justice major was once enrolled in one of my literature courses. Remote and taciturn, he sat in a back corner of the room each day and glowered into his textbook. His writing was hasty, flat, and clunky, typical of the kind of essays that, I knew from years of experience, had been labored over in the dead of night with a genuine hatred of the assignment, the course, and me. At the conclusion of the course, when each student was invited to write an anonymous evaluation, this young man (I recognized his handwriting) wrote that he had always disliked reading but now, after suffering through the course, he absolutely hated it. He admitted that he only enjoyed watching movies, ones in which "stuff blows up", and expressed relief that because he was going to become a police officer he'd never have to read or write again. Confessions like this horrify me. This young man—hostile and, yes, white—needed to take a literature course more than any other student I had ever encountered. The idea that I had potentially unleashed another angry white man into the world, one who was determined to enter law enforcement yet had a complete inability to empathize with people different from himself, sends tremors through my body to this day. He passed the course with a D.

Those ignorant of the ways black Americans have navigated through what bell hooks terms America's white racist capitalist patriarchy would do well to read the works of black authors. After reading *The Narrative of the Life of Frederick Douglass* in an

American literature course my freshman year of college, I vowed that I would spend a significant part of each day reading. A novel, a newspaper, the side of a cereal box—it didn't matter. How could I, an African American male, first generation college student from a downscale neighborhood with enough smarts to get into one of the top universities in the nation, shrug off my obligation to become as well-read as I could?

I'm not naive enough to think simply reading an acclaimed novel or a collection of poems by a black writer for thirty minutes a day will solve the problems of poverty, unemployment, racism, homophobia, HIV/AIDS, and gang violence among urban black youth. Yet I know that reading *Native Son* my senior year of high school and absorbing the poems of Nikki Giovanni and Yusef Komunyakaa, keeping a journal and writing my own poems, stories, novels, and essays, has kept me from bloodshed and death. Once, long ago, in utter despair, my choice in life was made startlingly clear to me—write or die. I think many black writers, at some point, have faced that same mortal choice. With each keystroke and every lash of the page, black writers assume the psychic and emotional landscape, however tortured or enraptured, of every black person who has begun or ended his or her life in the United States of America. We do not claim victimhood. We write to let the world know, without equivocation, that black literature simultaneously defines the black community and America and critiques both, opens its pages to the pleasures of the culture and its perils, makes room for all who seek its shelter and expels those who endeavor to assail us.

The arc of my life has propelled me toward a career in academia since I was a boy and delighted in reading and writing during playtime. Living alone with my grandparents forced me to find creative ways to amuse myself, and when I wasn't romping in my bedroom playing with action figures I read or watched television. I invented stories, acted out scenes from my favorite cartoons and sitcoms, and from time to time I attempted to commit some of my playtime hijinks to paper. My grandfather, an angry alcoholic born and bred in the Jim Crow South, never placed much stock in formal education, especially for a boy, and loudly objected to

What Color Is Your Hoodie?

the time I spent holed up in my bedroom reading and writing stories. I recall sitting at the desk in my bedroom once when I was a small boy simply copying text from a random book in cursive—a skill I learned from my cousin Chanda—and being seized by an irrational fear that I wouldn't be able to do homework once I grew up. Somehow I believed that once my formal education was over I would no longer have the chance to read or write. I was the only person I knew who derived pleasure from the utter mundane task of writing, from the feel of the pen in my hand as it glided across the stark white page, and I never wanted to lose it (the reality, now, that in our digital society we are moving farther and farther away from writing and that some elementary schools no longer teach cursive writing frightens me). At school I was a nerd, answering my teachers' questions even when it meant social suicide, completing assignments on time and earning high marks when boys were supposed to excel in athletics. The competing messages from my family—the women encouraging academic success; the men resolved that boys should only play sports—complicated my feelings toward both academics and sports. I could never truly take pride in the good grades I made because as a boy I wasn't supposed to care about books, yet my failure at sports compounded my feelings of inadequacy, and since academics was the area where I garnered the most praise it was where I focused my attention.

I enjoy working in academia because it is one of the few professions where one is paid to think and write, and frankly I am not qualified to earn a decent living in any other profession. Teaching is not without its frustrations, however. Working in the humanities presents challenges from anti-intellectual students and parents who continuously question the relevance of literature, history, philosophy and related disciplines, and pressure from administrators to lower the threshold for passing these courses. There is also competition from for-profit online schools that promise students degrees without the so-called hassles of taking and paying for classes such as these which they feel will have no impact on their lives or, more importantly, their future earning potential. This full scale assault on the humanities has, in recent years, disrupted pedagogical discourse, forced austerity in graduate admissions, and augmented requirements for tenure. Nevertheless, despite the ongoing changes, academia remains a field with much to offer people of color seeking to find ways to affect cultural and political change. Our presence in higher education—especially the presence of African American men, who are underrepresented throughout academia—imparts complex dimensions to every course we teach.

    I encounter a range of responses from students when I enter the classroom on the first day of class. I teach freshman level classes, and depending on what time of day my class is scheduled I can be the very first professor some students encounter in college. Most of the white students who attend Aurora University come from small towns and rural communities. Their parents on the whole are conservatives who revile academia and intellectuals, despise President Obama and all he stands for, and harbor deep suspicions of racial minorities, especially those in positions of authority. Although many of these students distance themselves from their families' opinions their worldview is nonetheless slanted toward a conservative ethos that has imperiled racial and sexual minorities in aggregate ways for generations. It never ceases to amaze me how these students, simply by virtue of being white, seem to think they are better at assessing their own work than I am. My white students are typically the ones who complain loudest when they fail to earn high grades, and they proffer abundant excuses when they don't turn in work or miss too many classes. If I don't change their grade—and I never do—they will whine and complain to their advisors, the dean, and even the president of the university until someone gives them what they want, yet no one ever does. It is primarily because of them that my syllabus expands semester after semester, growing with detailed disclaimers and provisos underscored or printed in bold type regarding attendance, late work, electronic submissions, and the like. This isn't to suggest that my black students aren't bratty and narcissistic, but my dynamic with them is markedly different. Black students have never accounted for more than one third of the students in any course I've taught at AU, and when they see me enter class on the first day they take immediate interest, sit up

What Color Is Your Hoodie?

straight and absorb every word I utter. In one class a small cluster of black students sitting in the back corner of the room actually applauded when I walked into the room on the first day of class and stood behind the podium, some of them exclaiming, "Yes!" and "All right!" Yet what troubles and saddens me about the black students is their readiness to give up. They maintain enthusiasm for the course until the first assignment is due, and if they don't make high marks, rather than seek guidance from me or visit a tutor, they simply stop trying. Many of them are among the first to drop my course, and some of them bypass the registrar's office altogether and instead of dropping the course officially merely stop coming to class, vanishing like apparitions with only their names penned in my grade book as evidence they were ever there.

These students haunt me because I was just like them upon entering Northwestern University. Although I was smart enough to gain admittance to one of the nation's most prestigious universities, my public school education (though far superior to the education most Aurora University's students acquire prior to entering college) in no way prepared me for the rigors of a university education. I went from taking classes where expectations were so low students passed if they regularly came to class to attending lectures with hundreds of students. As an engineering major with no head for science or higher order mathematics, I flunked out after freshman year but returned to Northwestern several years later committed to learning, and I excelled. In the midst of failing academically I had to confront my emerging homosexuality. Away from home from the first time and living among men, I, who had had such limited interactions with males up until then, could no longer deny my sexual attraction to men when I was housed with them, conversed with them, undressed with them, showered with them. and slept beside them. I suffered multiple shocks that year: being black and working class at a school where most students were white and affluent, struggling to adopt proper study habits and test taking skills when I never had to do so before, enduring separation from my family and environment for the first time, longing to express myself sexually with a man when I had been thoroughly convinced for years that I was heterosexual. At eighteen it was all too much to handle and when the university sent me a letter of dismissal at the end of the academic year subconsciously I knew leaving school was the best thing for me at the time.

My story mimic's the main character's struggles in ZZ Packer's deft short story "Drinking Coffee Elsewhere." I've taught Introduction to Literary Study every year for the last five years and each year I include "Drinking Coffee Elsewhere" on the syllabus. Without exception it has been my students' favorite short story each time I've taught the course because, like me, they can empathize with Dina's plight. A black girl from the ghettos of Baltimore, Dina makes her way to Yale, yet from the day she arrives on campus she immediately becomes prickly and misanthropic, hostile toward the entire community expect for a chubby white girl from Canada named Heidi who insinuates herself into the role of Dina's close friend despite Dina's initial objections. They work together in the dining hall, read together, even sleep together in the same bed. To Dina's surprise, yet not the reader's, Heidi eventually comes out as a lesbian and it is implied by other characters in the story that Dina may be gay as well. But unable to cope with the many stresses in her life, Dina drops out of Yale and returns to the ghetto to live with an aunt she barely knows, squandering her intellectual gifts and, from my perspective, shuddering herself further into the closet.

Packer's story taps into the insecurity, angst, and flux most people experience as they transition from childhood to adulthood. Dina's story is all too common at my university, especially among young men. With each passing year female enrollment at colleges and universities across the nation is increasing while enrollment among men is on the decline and shows no signs of reversing. The high female to male ratio of students I tutor, roughly eight to one, reflects this. The investment in higher education and the drive to obtain white collar jobs that will lift them into the middle class simply isn't a priority for many of the first generation college men at my university. For African American men, simply being admitted to a university is an accomplishment in itself, and if they flunk out or voluntarily choose to drop out they feel they've already

What Color Is Your Hoodie?

exceeded the expectations of their family and community by being alive, staying out of jail, and not impregnating anyone. They have achieved much more than any other male in their family has, so for them flunking out of college isn't a true failure. Yet from experience I know that black male students also carry a tremendous burden to succeed. When I was a freshman at Northwestern I lived every day petrified of failing. I had scores of people counting on me to earn a degree, obtain a high paying job, and rescue them from poverty. Coming from disadvantage and entering an environment of privilege intensifies any strive for success an individual has. My own dreams and desires, scholastic, personal and professional, had to be sacrificed for my mother's dream of me becoming a Fortune 500 CEO, motivated by the poverty and desperation that subsumed every moment of our lives. My grandparents and I once lived in a home where we had to fill a paint bucket full of water from the bath tub and pour it into the toilet because it wouldn't flush. Before school each morning I had to shake my coat to make sure no roaches had crawled inside. I went from that environment to taking classes in vector calculus and writing critical essays on novels by Nathaniel Hawthorne and James Fenimore Cooper. When I told my mother I wanted to be a writer she gave me a conciliatory smile and said, "Oh, you mean a journalist?" My freshman year in college was never really about me because I was not really present in any decisions I made. The true me had not emerged yet; I had no voice, so others spoke for me and made up my mind for me. I did what I thought everyone else wanted and expected me to do and because of it I failed in every conceivable way.

Now that I am an educator, as I plan my syllabus for African American Literature, I wonder what taking this same course my freshman year at Northwestern would have done for me. Upon my return to the university many years later as an English major I had the opportunity to take several courses in African American literature, African American studies, gender studies, and gay and lesbian history. Three of my professors were black men. Whether they were gay or not I've no idea, but I have assumptions. They were dynamic instructors who, to me, seemed enamored of their pedagogy and could declaim theories, philosophies, paradigms, and histories as if they were reciting nursery rhymes. Unlike some of their white colleagues who would wear ragged, grungy clothes to class, they always attended class stylishly dressed in trousers, a button down shirt and tie, accessorizing with a fedora or a tie pin or silver cufflinks shined to a bright luster. For me, a student who still, at twenty-seven, felt out of place, this time because I was gay and older than most undergraduates, studying black masculinity in a university course taught by a black man helped me come into my own as a black man and made me value and assert my manhood in a way I never had before. Watching a black man with dark skin and dreadlocks stand before a roomful of white students and me, the only black student in the class, and masterfully lecture about the myriad themes present in Virginia Woolf's *Jacob's Room* squelched any self-reproach I experienced over my interest in British literature. Learning about the Niagara Convention and the Freedom Riders from a black man not much older than me whose passion for justice and civil rights was so palpable students openly apologized to him when they missed a class helped me chart a new destiny for myself. If I could be like them, I reasoned as I sat in their classes, I would have it. And I didn't even know what "it" was.

* * *

I am not out to my students, and I have several reasons for not disclosing my sexual orientation to them. First, I believe that in our current age there is entirely too much familiarity and informality, particularly when it comes to the details of one's private life. Unlike Baby Boomers who passionately challenged authority on the basis of sound, critical arguments, Millennials will not even acknowledge authority figures, the power they possess, or their own lack of power. They have been raised to bring everyone in authority down to their level or puff themselves up to the level of authority figures. Their inflated, unearned self-confidence has spawned an ongoing cultural discussion since the millennium began. Today's college students, consumed with Facebook, Twitter, and texting, readily divulge,

WHAT COLOR IS YOUR HOODIE?

to their detriment, the private details of their lives to anyone and expect others to do the same. Some professors, either out of fear of the impact bad evaluations will have on their chances of gaining tenure or merely out of an emotional need to be accepted, do their best to befriend students and yield to their requests rather than take the strong stance an educator must assume and do the rough work of teaching them and assessing their work in a detached, unbiased manner. As the head writing tutor for the university I've sat with the students of just about every full-time, visiting, or pro-rata professor on campus. I know their teaching philosophies, their rapport with students both in and out of the classroom and their expectations, to say nothing of the details of their personal lives. Without question, gay and lesbian professors, and straight professors who have aligned themselves with queer politics or queer theory, set much higher expectations for their students, grade papers meticulously, write and publish more books and articles, attend more conferences, and invest more time planning lectures and serving on committees than their peers. From bell hooks to Dwight McBride, Eve Sedgwick to Michel Foucault, queer/feminist scholars and theorists have reshaped the humanities in the last thirty years. I've often wondered if these professors are overcompensating, that the rigorous demands they place on themselves derive from a need to prove themselves; a way of telling colleagues, administrators, students, and anyone else who dares to challenge them that their sexual orientation or gender will not be an obstacle to achieving their career ambitions.

If my students knew I was gay suddenly their focus wouldn't be on their studies; rather, they'd spend all class period thinking about me sucking dick. That's a vulgar exaggeration of course, yet when students become preoccupied with their instructors' private lives, particularly those of us who live alternative lifestyles, learning becomes static and very little can reactivate it. When I began teaching years ago it became apparent, from my own experiences and those I've heard from colleagues at AU and other institutions, that professors who are not straight white men of a certain age must fight for respect and control in their classes, particularly women of color. As much as I would like to contribute personal experience when gay and lesbian themes present in assigned readings and class discussions, I know doing so would prejudice the discussion and jeopardize my power in the class. Although I know several gay professors who are out to their students, they teach courses such as psychology or social work, or they teach at other institutions which boast a more liberal-minded student population. Disclosing their sexual orientation can do them no harm and in some instances it benefits the class and helps prepare students for work in service fields. I teach freshman who are not English majors; they take my courses as general education requirements. The business administration, nursing, and physical education majors who fight to stay awake during discussions of "Battle Royal" and "Everyday Use," like the criminal justice major who authored a screed against me and my literature course, want to "D it out" and move on. I believe wholeheartedly that all students should be exposed to the full panoply of experience a university education has to offer, even when it comes from encountering individuals unlike themselves. This is among the many gifts of diversity in the classroom. Yet as a black gay professor at a small university where I am not eligible for tenure, where I tutor students who still refer to African Americans as colored people in their essays, and the retired white homeowners who live directly across the street from campus drive cars with bumper stickers that read, "Don't Blame Me, I Voted For the American," I must carefully weigh the benefit of coming out against the cost it will have on my professional stature.

    Complicating all of this is the second reason I will not come out to students: my husband also teaches at the same university. Tenured, white, and fiftysomething, Gerald earned his PhD in history the year we met. He has been teaching at Aurora University for fifteen years now and currently has the distinction of being one of the longest serving professors at the university. I seldom think of myself as a true academic in the way Gerald is an academic; rather, I am a creative writer who happens to earn a living working within academia. My work responsibilities stop at the end of spring semester and do not resume until fall semester. In the faculty and staff hierarchy at Aurora University my name occupies a space precipitously low

What Color Is Your Hoodie?

on the list, but Gerald ranks among the university's most valuable employees, and his record speaks for itself. To date he has published two well-received books, countless articles and reviews, coordinated panels and conferences, led committees, and even served as dean for a year. Colleagues and administrators esteem him and students regard him with both admiration and fear. At least once a semester a student will ask Gerald if he once served in the military, given his drill sergeants' steely, brusque persona in the classroom and his penchant for regimentation. In the world of academia my husband is living the dream. Yet until I came to work for the university he kept his private life strictly guarded. Our friends and colleagues at work, as far as either of us knows, have not outed us to students, though I've no doubt they whisper and question; perhaps they rout the Internet for any morsel of information concerning our private life they can nibble on. Gerald and I never interact with one another on campus; we work in different departments on opposite ends of the campus, so we seldom run into each other. If I were to come out to students I would be pulling Gerald out of the closet as well, and like me he simply has no wish to conflate his personal and professional lives any more than they already have been. Our work identities protect our private lives and interests. To chip away at those personages would expose our love to unimagined risk.

* * *

Like most people in their early twenties, my second cousins Jimí and Niecie broadcast the major events of their lives on Facebook. Typically they comment on the ups and downs of dating in Kansas City complete with relationship triumphs, woes, and a broad scale of ghetto drama. They hold nothing back, posting challenges to rivals who seek to steal away their lovers while firmly asserting their position as dominant females who will stop at nothing to protect their happy homes. My young cousins never cease to impress me; their candor and self-esteem oppose the wilting docility exemplified by many women in our family. While I, unlike them, customarily save bombasts for my journal, I'm glad they have Facebook as a forum to express themselves in an unabashed, public manner. In my eyes they fear nothing, truly making them products of their generation.

Jimí and Niecie are lesbians.

Having already relocated to Chicago at the time they came out, I wasn't there to find out our family's reaction to their sexuality. In an email some time ago Niecie asked me when I knew I was gay, what prompted me to come out and how our family reacted. I responded with the following:

When did I come out? Well, it happened this way: It was late 1996. I was 22 and I hadn't been involved with anybody, male or female. I was still trying to figure out whether or not I was gay. I was living with Granny, working full-time at Bartle Hall and part-time at Blockbuster, and my life was pretty much working, coming home and watching movies. Then one day I met a guy (he was older), had sex with him, and then I knew for sure I was gay.

I started going out to gay bars and meeting new people. I don't know if you remember but at the time my mother and Steve [my stepfather] were living in Iowa. She would phone Granny and ask her how I was doing and Granny told her lots of guys kept calling the house, guys who weren't the friends who usually called the house. That's not all—I started dating my first boyfriend, and I'd usually come home on Fridays after work, shower and change, then leave and not come home until Saturday afternoon. Then I'd change clothes, leave again, and not come home until Sunday at dinner time. So of course all the women in the family started talking. They guessed that if I was staying out all night I must be spending those nights with a certain someone, yet they assumed it was a woman. Only our cousin Alexis knew the truth, and she wasn't talking to anybody (she's still my rock and my homegirl!) One Sunday afternoon, Aunt Shirley rushed into my bedroom and shut the door. She was frantic and on the verge of tears. She asked me if I was gay, and when I told her that I was and showed her a picture of my then boyfriend she was crushed. She said she'd pray for me. She did even more—every morning when I went out to my car I'd find little pamphlets from church under my car windshield like, "God Doesn't Want You to Be Gay" and "Learn

What Color Is Your Hoodie?

to Live a Christian Life." Mama called a few days later and, without ever bringing up my sexuality, said that she has always been proud of me, she'll always be proud of me and all she's ever wanted for me was to be happy. That was that.

Honestly, I think I was the only person on Earth who didn't know I was gay. I think most people were just waiting for me to figure things out. From the time I was a kid I've always been the weird one in the family, which is a good thing because being the weird gay guy in the family probably saved me from ending up dead or in jail. I mean my parents were 14 and 15 when I was born and I lived with my grandparents; Granddaddy was a drunk and Granny suffered from depression. The men in the family have never disrespected me but they haven't necessarily gone out of their way to include me. I sometimes feel cheated because all the boys in our family were born after I was all grown up. The only time I really experienced homophobia from the family was when David Allen gave that hateful speech at Shirley and David's 25th wedding anniversary a few years back. He made a blatantly homophobic comment and I got so mad I walked out. I wrote Shirley a letter about it and she was very apologetic. She told me that she eventually came around and the Dave was young (he had just started seeing Tori at the time and she felt Tori was a bad influence on him) and still trying to find his way in the world. She and David spoke to Dave about the situation but he and I have never been close since. But I think the one thing that has made everyone at ease with my gayness is that fact that #1: I've been with Gerald for 15 years and #2: I'm not swishy and queeny. Honestly, I'm a very boring person. But I can't tell you how much Mama and Lexy have helped me. Their support and yours has really meant so much. My mother and I practically grew up together—remember, she was 14—and without her, and Granny before her, I probably would be dead or in jail. Seriously.

If you and Jimi can learn anything from me I hope you learn that it's okay to take risks in life and that you have to do what makes you happy. The culture is different now than it was when I came out and the family is much more supportive now than they were back then. We're all older—I'll be 40 in 2 years!—and we all realize that life *is too short for pettiness. I'm so happy you and Jimi have so much support and that you're taking care of yourselves. Always take care of yourself, physically, emotionally, and financially. Learn. Read. Express yourself. There is a rich, wonderful history of black lesbian and gay men you both need to learn about. I need to send you some books.*

I'm very proud of you! Every day I read one of your posts I feel the whole family has accomplished something extraordinary. Please keep taking risks. Keep learning and keep being who you really are!

The incident I refer to in my letter involving my cousin Dave remains the one and only time homophobia aimed directly at me came from the lips of a family member, one who I had considered a little brother when he was born and I was nine years old. At an anniversary dinner which should have been a celebration of his parents' lasting commitment, where family and friends who had supported them and their family over the years should have felt welcome and safe, I and other queers in the room, both out and closeted, suffered a scathing attack. It occurred in a poem Dave wrote and recited before a crowd of roughly fifty people. While I cannot recall this lines verbatim the sentiment he conveyed was that his parents' "biblical" marriage had endured for so long because they were living according to God's plan, not like gays and lesbians who were by their very nature openly defying God's law. This incident took place in the summer of 2005, a defining year in Gay Rights. Only months before, President Bush had begun his second term, skirted into office after a campaign orchestrated by Karl Rove that utilized same-sex marriage as a wedge issue to drive conservatives into the voting booth. The previous year Massachusetts become the first state in the nation to legalize same-sex marriage, and in pop culture a spate of gay-themed films and television shows, chief among them the landmark film *Brokeback Mountain*, were about to be released. Tensions across the nation strained as familial ties and friendships, divided by fanatical political partisanship, ossified. Dave's comments were in essence the echo of talking points from Fox News.

But I wasn't about to let him get away with it. Thankfully, my

WHAT COLOR IS YOUR HOODIE?

aunt and uncle had an open mic at the ceremony so that friends and family could stand up and share their thoughts and feelings about their special wedding anniversary. After Dave finished his poem (which hurt me all the more since no one in the family had ever begun to write poetry until I did and found success with it) I approached the microphone and, as tactfully as I could, leveled a pointed rejoinder to Dave's homophobic comments. I told the crowd of family and friends that I was proud to have been included in my aunt and uncle's anniversary celebration, that deep, abiding love as they have experienced is difficult to achieve and must always be celebrated. I reminisced about my childhood with them, a time before their children were born when they served as surrogate parents for me while my mother grew into womanhood and my father found his manhood in the embrace of a family he began with another woman before he endured a short stint in prison. Then I made my stinging indictment: I informed Dave and all who gathered in the hotel ballroom that in the current cultural climate of intolerance and partisan gamesmanship we shouldn't forget, in light of my aunt and uncle's happy marriage, that untold numbers of men and women cannot legally marry because of the intense homophobia which has poisoned our culture. I named no names; I called no one out. I merely spoke for those who had been wounded by Dave's ignorant comments, millions of men and women like myself who are so often invited to family gatherings yet are not truly included in the festivities; the ones mailed an invitation to a wedding yet aware that they cannot bring the person who means more to them than anyone else, whispered about behind their backs; the ones who sit alone in the corner of the ballroom while everyone else dances and laughs, the ones who must pretend they don't hear the drunk uncle or aunt make a joke about fags with gerbils stuck up their ass, dikes getting wherever they need to go "lickety split," queers flaming into death. I felt only a brief moment of satisfaction after my remarks before one of my aunt and uncle's friends, a well dressed middle aged black man who I swear was cruising me before dinner, approached the mic when I sat down and echoed Dave's homophobic stance. It was then I got up from the table and left the hotel. My relationship with Dave has been frosty ever since.

    In the years since I relocated to the Chicago area with Gerald, and especially since I became a university instructor, I've come to realize that teaching does not end when I leave the classroom. Not only am I teaching young adults at school what it means to be black, I am teaching blacks and the rest of society what it means to be gay. Like so many other gays and lesbians my age, when I was coming of age I had no gay role models. I knew nothing of Stonewall, gay subculture or our community's prolonged fight for equality. The host of gays and lesbians in pop culture today and the number of gay celebrities who have come out of the closet wasn't the reality Gen X and older generations of gays lived in. Living my life as I have with my husband at my side, maintaining a home with him, presenting one another at family gatherings, and expanding our circle of friends and acquaintances demonstrates to my family members—those who support my lifestyle and those who rail against it—that gays should not be feared or shunned and that our lives, just as theirs, contribute to the common good of society. Jimí and Niecie look to me to model a healthy, productive life as a homosexual, something no one did for me when I was discovering my homosexuality.

    The toxicity of homophobia in the black community has been a topic of impassioned dialogue for as long as I can remember. I use the word *toxicity* here on purpose, for the calumny and sheer malice some blacks direct at gays and lesbians poisons the entire community, manifests in fractures within family, contributes to loss of labor and home and, perhaps more lethal than anything else, accelerates the spread of HIV/AIDS within the community. The work Harlem Renaissance writers and artists did to expose the invidiousness of homophobia and sexism within the black community has not slowed since the 1920s. Artists and intellectuals from James Baldwin to bell hooks to Keith Boykin and Melissa Harris-Perry have written and spoken at length about the corrosiveness of homophobia, how it can retard and even undo the strides blacks have made since the Civil Rights era. Yet it seems no matter how many black men and women come out of the closet and loudly proclaim their right to love and equality, regardless of

What Color Is Your Hoodie?

the increasing number of gay and lesbian blacks who populate films and television shows and help relax some of the fear others have of us, and against their better judgment, many African Americans remain adamant and strident in their opposition to gay rights. Like my cousin Dave, those blacks swathed in Christian fundamentalism, much like their white counterparts on the fringe of the Republican Party, would rather see the entire race obliterated than abandon their hatred and invite us a place at the table.

To live as a dual minority, to belong to two groups constantly under attack in Western culture, gives black gays and lesbians the unique opportunity to educate, for each moment we live our lives, write our stories, protest for just causes and claim space, we prove our power and worth and strengthen our communities. It is impossible for us to avoid teaching moments: instances where we are called upon, whether we want to or not, to correct a misapprehension, right a wrong, give a voice to those who are voiceless and provide safe havens. We harness our mutual reserves of fortitude, endurance, charity, and forgiveness, and simply by living honorably, with joy, zeal, and pride, we embolden others to claim their own true selves, to love and to heal.

Baldwin Boys and Harris Homies

Several months ago, desperate to surround myself with black gay writers, who could better relate to my work, I placed an ad online to establish a black gay writers group. My goal was to start a monthly writers circle in which black gay men engaged in any type of writing project could receive helpful criticism from members of their community, the ones who would best comprehend the aesthetics and themes embodied in their work. The idea of creating a community of well-read black gay men who were articulate, witty, creative, disciplined, and skilled in the craft of writing had been on my mind since I earned a masters of fine arts in writing five years earlier. At that time I was the only African American student in the program and one of its few openly gay students. My peers, who were for the most part white middle class young adults, seemed to have very little cultural engagement with the black community beyond listening to popular hip-hop songs and watching a few Will Smith movies. Although some of them took an active interest in my writing, others professed their ignorance of black history and culture and expressed no interest in my work. On one occasion a pedigreed, well-educated classmate who fancied himself the star of the writing program wrote me a three-page letter conveying his disinclination to read the first draft of my novel, which I had submitted to our workshop, only to relay to me that upon hearing our classmates' encouraging reviews he decided to peruse it after all. Following this admission he provided an exhaustive list of the many ways he believed my novel failed before dismissing it as a weak attempt to fuse *Native Son* and *Will & Grace*. Expressions of condescension like this were actually quite common in my workshops, and because of them my experience in the program left me jaded and more self-conscious about my writing than I was before I entered graduate school.

After I earned my MFA and tried to secure agent representation for my novel, the litany of rejections I received sent me into a downward spiral. Agents deemed the novel either too black or too gay. While the shelves of my local bookstores continued to stock one clichéd, poorly written mass market novel after another, my brainchild gathered dust on my desk, all two hundred and twenty-three pages yellowing. Many of the African American novels being published at the time were those deemed street lit: fiction focused on baby mama drama, church girls in love with thugs, and the general hoopla of ghetto life. The only gay novels being published involved eighteen-year-old blond white boys from Nebraska who become models in New York City and end up living fabulous lives with older rich boyfriends while participating in one orgy after another. Finding my style of writing and my personal experiences reflected in both black and gay novels proved futile. Yet I believed whole-heartedly that somewhere in Chicago existed other black gay writers like me who were committed to writing and wanted to make their mark in American letters. When I posted the call for my group on Meetup.com, I described it as a place where black gay men who were serious about writing could gather once a month to workshop each other's work, trade information on getting published or finding jobs, and perhaps even hold open mic readings. Six men joined; only one showed up.

Landon and I met on a chilly, wet Sunday afternoon in February at a coffee shop in Boystown. Impish, effete, and soft spoken, he shook my hand, sat down at the table with me and soon we began exchanging stories about how we came to be writers, hardships we've encountered teaching disinterested undergraduates the finer points of composition, and our challenges getting published. Landon self-published a slim collection of poems a few years ago and presented me with an autographed copy. In exchange I gave him a chapter from a novella I had written a few years ago that I've been thinking about expanding into a novel. We got along very

What Color Is Your Hoodie?

well in that first meeting and agreed to meet again the following month to discuss one another's work and exchange new material. Over the next three months we met at the same coffee shop on the last Sunday of each month and offered insights into each other's writing, hoping other members would gradually show up and take part. We conversed through text messages and emails and eventually became comfortable enough with each other for Landon to discuss a burgeoning fling that had begun between him and an older man he recently met at a bus stop. I write fiction, essays, and poetry, but Landon only writes poems. I read his book of poems, and although I didn't think they were the most accomplished or technically proficient poems I'd ever read, they were bold confessional works, stark in presentation, and frank in subject matter. The collection chronicled his ongoing battle with HIV, the physical and psychological toll the virus and its treatment took on his body, and the ups and downs he experienced dating black gay men as a black gay man with HIV. Short, blunt, and esoteric, Landon's poems privileged subject over style, technique and acuity of language, recalling the hastily written, overemotional knock-offs of better poems that I and virtually every poet wrote at the beginning of his or her career. Landon had a trove of personal experiences, feelings, and opinions he wanted to express, but he still had a long way to go as a poet. I myself had taken a personal vow at the end of my MFA program never to workshop my poems again. For me, fiction and essays are labors of creative expression, and I can withstand criticism of that work in a way I cannot tolerate the butchering of my poems, which I view as labors of love. Good or bad, any critique of my poetry leaves me feeling awkward or, in extreme cases, utterly destroyed.

In April, National Poetry Month, I decided to follow Landon's lead and attempt to write a poem each day for the entire month. Although I was swamped at work, writing a poem each night became a task I looked forward to, a way to relieve the day's stress. Before long, several interesting motifs began to emerge in these poems: trains, boxcars, departing for the open road, the conflation of writing and history, eroticism—all figured into these poems, some of the best I felt I had ever written. Landon and I agreed to exchange our poems and discuss them at our next meeting. His new poems departed from confessionals to meditations on African American pop culture. Specifically, his poems made pointed criticisms of *Good Times, Sanford and Son,* and *The Cosby Show*. Though his poems conveyed praise and a sense of solidarity with the working class characters of *Good Times* and *Sanford and Son*, he lambasted *The Cosby Show* for what he perceived as the Huxtables' upper-middle class snobbery and abandonment of the race. The poems both angered and perplexed me, yet I had to put whatever personal feelings I had aside and critique the work on its own merits, or lack thereof. When we met at the coffee shop, I chose my words carefully when I offered my critique of Landon's verse. As always, I began with the aspects of the collection I admired and felt warranted praise before I shared my critique and misgivings of the poems' themes and style, which in some cases was quite superficial and solipsistic (he had a habit of purposely leaving his poems untitled then dedicating them to various people). My biggest criticism of Landon's poems regarded his hostile attitude toward *The Cosby Show* and its characters. In so many words, he reviled the Huxtables as white folks in black face, sell-outs and race traitors of the worst variety. These were not poems; they were screeds against the black middle class, and I communicated this to Landon as tactfully as I could.

    He accepted my opinions calmly and politely, gathered the pages I had scribbled with green ink, and then began to discuss the thirty or so poems I had written. When I glanced down at the pages he had annotated I noticed lots of question marks, but I dismissed them. Landon and I had both endured the rigors of writing workshops, and in spite of my apprehension toward seeking criticism of my poems, I felt with Landon that I was in safe company. I didn't expect him to praise these rough drafts to the heavens, I had no grand illusions about them, yet I could not have prepared myself for the vituperative comments he was about to make. Initially, he asked me lots of questions about some of the references I made in the poems, those pertaining to Greek mythology ("Who are Zeus

What Color Is Your Hoodie?

and Ganymede?"), food and wine ("What is a gimlet?") and classic cinema ("Who was Greta Garbo?") Next, he questioned some of my word choices, confessing that he had to consult his dictionary several times during the process of reading the poems. In general he felt the poems were too "clean;" for example, in the few erotic poems included among my offerings, he suggested a flurry of synonyms I should use for *semen*, and balked at many of the linguistic flourishes I utilized in the poems. These last criticisms were quite valid and I took them into consideration during the process of revision. Yet after our meeting I flipped through my poems and became enraged as I read his comments, which gradually devolved from constructive criticisms to calumnious personal attacks: *Why aren't you writing about the black experience? Are you still a brutha? You just don't want to be black. The black aesthetic is beautiful—find it!* Landon attacked virtually every poem I had written that wasn't overtly sexual or didn't directly address race. The sharp criticisms I received in my writing program were tiny thorns compared to Landon's poisoned arrows.

My experience with Landon left me reeling for weeks. I consulted a few other black gay writers I know in other parts of the country and asked them how to handle the situation with him. Without exception each man urged me to cut off the relationship. One peer opined that Landon and I come from opposing cultural, political, and ideological spectrums of the African American community, and although each of us was engaged in artistic projects that were worthy and necessary I would never change his ideas, nor he mine. Though I hesitated, I eventually sent Landon an email claiming that due to the shortage of members in our group I felt it was best to shut down the website and go our separate ways.

Until recently American society has been loathed to openly discuss class. This changed at the beginning of the twenty-first century when the Bush-Gore battle over the White House illuminated the red state-blue state divide between Americans, revealing cultural and class tensions that hitherto simmered beneath the surface. Now, in the strangling grip of the Great Recession, Americans' awareness of class differences and cultural distinctions couldn't be more obvious. Democrat vs. Republican, wine vs. beer, city vs. country, Smart Cars vs. SUVs, cultural schisms in the United States lay bare for citizens of all regions and demographics to debate, defend, and debunk. Those of us who pride ourselves on being culturally aware recognize that no group is a monolith. Democrats come in many strips, as do Republicans. Black in the South distinguish themselves from Northern blacks through language, dialect, dress, and other regionalisms. The black community in the twenty-first century, more politically and economically powerful now than at any other time in its long history in the United States, continues to expose the nation and the world to its wonderfully rich, diverse culture. Though the nation has been slow to embrace the Gay Rights Movement, in recent years it has gained momentum, evidenced primarily by same-sex marriage victories in seventeen states and the District of Columbia. Gays and lesbians environ every political, economic, and social sphere, yet I believe the dominant culture refuses to view gays as a diverse population. For them, Rosie O'Donnell represents all lesbians and Carson Kressley epitomizes all gay men. In my view, diminishing the scope of homosexuality makes it much easier for homophobes to attack the LGBT community and more difficult for gays and lesbians to break out of stereotypical tropes.

Some place the origins of the black gay male aesthetic in the Harlem Renaissance, where literary luminaries Langston Hughes, Countee Cullen, Wallace Thurman, and Richard Bruce Nugent founded a literary and artistic style replicated by today's authors. In the years following the Second World War in what many consider the most culturally and politically conservative period in US history, there was a shift in black arts, one more stridently political and radical than had been previously celebrated during the Harlem Renaissance. It was during this era that author James Baldwin rose to prominence. Baldwin's work protests racism, subsumes the full breadth of African American culture, and unapologetically embraces homosexuality. Influenced by the works of Henry James and his own excursions throughout Europe, Baldwin's work is artful, nuanced, and highly literate. Unlike some authors of the Harlem Renaissance era who discussed sexuality in their work remained coy on the subject of their own sexuality, Baldwin was the first black literary giant who openly disclosed his homosexuality and demanded the world accept him, all parts of him, for who he was. James Baldwin remained America's most notable black gay writer and since his death in 1987 has had the mantel of black gay elder statesman bestowed upon him by contemporary black gay writers and artists.

In the 1990s, author E. Lynn Harris gained notoriety with his first novel, *Invisible Life*. Though born in Flint, Michigan, Harris was raised in the South and remained a Southern boy at heart all his life. Like Baldwin his novels candidly explore the lives and struggles of gay and bisexual African American men. Harris' frank writing style and his willingness to expose previously taboo topics such as homophobia within the black church and down low behavior among straight-identified black men resonated throughout the black community and, like Baldwin, earned him both praise and scorn from African Americans across political, social, and intellectual terrains.

Comparisons between Baldwin and Harris abound, yet a closer look reveals that these two authors couldn't be more different. While Baldwin's characters migrate from the Deep South to New York City and various European locals, Harris locates his characters squarely within urban sections of the United States. Baldwin's heroes engage in sexual relationships with white men and women; Harris's characters maintain relationships exclusively with other African Americans. As concerns sexual intimacy in his works, Baldwin either hints at it or uses rococo descriptions to convey it to readers. Harris, on the other hand, never shies away from an opportunity to expose his readers to sex, especially same sex couplings; his language and descriptions are graphic and titillating. Perhaps the main difference between these authors is their approach to writing in general. Owing to a childhood in which books became his constant companions, Baldwin's writing is controlled, elevated, and highly literate. By contrast, Harris' writing is relaxed: he floods is novels with urban vernacular and crafts characters and plots that are inspired by torrid daytime soap operas. Even some of the titles of his novels (*What Becomes of the Broken Hearted*, *I Say a Little Prayer*) are borrowed from popular R&B hits, localizing his work in a black urban sensibility. Though many black and gay readers and scholars celebrate Harris as Baldwin's twenty-first century scion, this appellation is hastily applied and diminishes the individual contributions of both authors.

I have long held the belief that black gay men can be placed in two general categories: Baldwin boys and Harris homies. While race, gender, and sexual orientation serve as their nexus, each group, like rival fraternities, promotes an ethos and aesthetic in opposition to its counterpart. Baldwin boys are often accused of being race traitors; they use proper English, date outside of their race, travel abroad, read lofty books, watch art house and foreign language films, listen to jazz and classical music and buy their clothes from stores like Banana Republic. Harris homies date black men exclusively, watch BET and Tyler Perry films, attend church regularly, groove to hip hop, gospel, and R&B, wear oversized T-shirts and baggy jeans. Although these designations are by no means rigidly adhered to, they broadly identify the aesthetic cultural markers of black gay men in America. Dissimilarity among black gay men also extends geographically: just as blacks in the South have a cultural ethos distinct from those who live on the East coast or in the Southwest, black gay men differ by region. Brothers in Washington, DC environ either Dupont Circle or northern Virginia. The contrast between brothers in Oakland and San Francisco is quite obvious to those who live in northern California. In Chicago a definite schism exists between black gay men who live in upscale North Side neighborhoods and those who live within the Black Belt on the South Side. The conglomeration of black gay men into two distinct cliques prompts multiple questions among them: Are Harris homies more black than Baldwin boys? Do Baldwin boys have more education and higher income? Do Harris homies have bad credit? Do Baldwin boys hate their race? Are Harris homies really in denial of their homosexuality? Do Baldwin boys consider themselves black first or gay first? Unchallenged, these absurd questions become insults. We call each other wanna-be thugs and stuck-up Oreos, Sambos and Uncle Toms. The epithets we hurl at each other signify not only the insidiousness of racism and homophobia but the self-injury black gay men as a whole suffer and commit each day. Primarily, education and class are the issues that wedge the members of our community. A black gay man's ability or inability to access one or both of them shapes his cultural identity and his engagement with others. Yet more than any other issue, the question of racial allegiance centralizes the friction between these two groups, with Harris homies casting aspersions on Baldwin boys' commitment to the black race who, in turn, affirm their right to express blackness in their own way while simultaneously deriding Harris homies for taking such a narrow and, frankly, essentialist position on race. The fact of our common heritage and sexual orientation does little, it seems, to unify black gay men. We are of the same, yet we are not the same.

People are different and cultures are different, but what good does it do to highlight these differences, especially when doing so can potentially broaden the schism between them? The simple answer to this question is that celebrating difference is important, especially in a society that is becoming increasingly homogenous through corporatization. No two people are the same and no two black gay men's experiences are the same. The United States thrives on difference and brazenly trumpets its singularity across the globe, yet our culture, just like every other culture, hypocritically demands conformity among its citizens in every possible way. We insist immigrants speak fluent English and adopt our individualistic Horatio Alger personal philosophy. The dominant culture regularly punishes citizens who are not white, male, Christian, heterosexual, wealthy, and able bodied. Social movements inspired by women, racial and sexual minorities, and the working class have advanced identity politics in the United States, yet these groups still cope with discrimination. The rise of women into positions of power in politics, academia, finance, and other professions has not eliminated sexism, which still pervades every socioeconomic area of society decades after the first wave of feminism swept the nation. The African American community continues to fight for equality and an end to racial discrimination in spite of Barack Obama's presidency and the ascension of blacks into the middle and upper economic classes. Those who inhabit the LGBT community enjoy more freedom and acceptance now than ever before, yet in most states anti-gay legislation fails to safeguard gays and lesbians against workplace discrimination, hate crimes, and other abuses. Achievements made by a few members of a group do not erase the brutal reality from which the group as a whole still suffers.

The black gay community, like all groups, mirrors variances in class, and the result is a community as multicultural as the entire US population, steeped in tradition and subject to the same biases as other groups. Black gay men risk internalizing the racist, homophobic ethos of the culture whenever we refuse to support and embrace one another regardless of our differences and choose instead to see each other as pretentious snobs wearing Banana Republic ties or ill-mannered thugs plodding around in Timberland boots. A critical scene in Marlon Rigg's 1989 documentary *Tongues Untied* illustrates adversarial relationships among some black gay men. Riggs quotes Joseph Beam's "Brother to Brother: Words from the Heart" in voice over, recalling walking down Castro Street and encountering another black gay men walking in the opposite direction. The men had previously met and spoken to each other several times at a local gay club, yet when he approached Riggs the other man averted his eyes and passed him as if they were complete strangers. Failing to recognize members of one's own community ("You ain't gon speak?) is an unforgivable betrayal among black men regardless of sexual orientation or class. A nod of the head accompanied by a slightly whispered, "'Sup?" serves as currency among black men more valuable than silver or gold. This gesture—practiced only by African American men and a source of envy and endless fascination among men of other races—informs black men that no matter what our station in life, regardless of our differences, pasts, success, or failures, we belong, flesh and spirit, to this group. United by a history of bondage, lynching, degradation, and disenfranchisement, African American men share a bond so sacrosanct that to openly discuss our tacit codes of identification, even in these pages, is tantamount to heresy. The

What Color Is Your Hoodie?

loss of brotherhood, I know from personal experience, is a common fear among gay youths, as is the feeling that no one else in the world is like them. When I first realized that I was attracted to men (I wasn't yet prepared to call myself gay, for I believe the term *gay* connotes alliance with social, political, and historical systems that I, a sheltered adolescent, wasn't ready to make) one of my biggest fears was that I would be all alone, ostracized from my community and loved ones. In my environment, no one was like me. One of the many wonderful aspects of gay culture is the unyielding support we give to one another, even to gay men we may not know. At the height of the AIDS crisis, which all but decimated an entire generation of gay men, those who suffered from the disease relied on an extensive support network. Scores of men throughout the community took turns feeding, bathing, comforting, and assisting those afflicted with the disease any way they could, whether they were close friends, passing acquaintances, or perfect strangers. In writing this essay I am constantly reminded of a phrase that resounds throughout every region of black gay America: brother to brother. The last thing black gay men should do is make enemies of one another. Racism and homophobia are as widespread and toxic today as they were when Hughes, Nugent, and their contemporaries were forging the black gay male world we all now inhabit. Even as the members of the Harlem Renaissance squabbled among themselves, embarked on their own literary projects, failed or succeed as artists, and faced their own personal demons, they never wavered in their support and acceptance of one another, collaborating on the publication of *Fire!!* and defending one another publicly in interviews. In the decades following the Harlem Renaissance, when James Baldwin rose to literary prominence, Langston Hughes had become the most recognizable and celebrated member of the Harlem Renaissance and the nation's most esteemed black poet. Though Hughes and Baldwin occasionally took umbrage with each other's work, they admired one another because they realized that their individual projects and commitment to civil rights contributed to a much larger project, one surpassing the expansion of civil rights, literature, or identity politics. I like to think that if Baldwin had lived to read

E. Lynn Harris' works he would have embraced Harris in the same way Harris embraced Baldwin's work and credited both Baldwin and Hughes for paving the way for him as a black gay writer. In the final analysis, the methods employed to gain visibility are not so important. What is important is that black gay men as a group gain visibility and control of our representation to mitigate the struggle for tolerance for not only our brothers but for all people.

When I recount my experiences with Landon, ambivalence weighs heavily upon me. I had been searching for my true literary peers for quite a long time and felt overwhelmingly discouraged that in a city as large as Chicago I could only find one black gay man who shared my devotion to creative writing. Though we weren't completely simpatico, Landon was one of my own, my contemporary, my ally, my brother. His unwillingness to accept me for who I am and his essentialist view of blackness—limited to ghetto, working class, anti-white African American art and experience—wounded me deeply. But I cannot place all the blame for the demise of our kinship on Landon. I blame myself as much as him for severing our line of communication. Seeking to avoid a potentially ugly confrontation, I summarily cut off all contact with Landon rather than sit down with him brother to brother and have a thorough discussion of our respective poetry collections. We may not have had a meeting of the minds, and we probably would have ended our association anyway, but at least Landon would have been given an opportunity to explain his comments. He could have better articulated his animus toward the black middle-class and black gay men like me. I denied him the chance to explain why he harbors suspicions about us and why he feels abandoned by us. I feel the same way. I didn't give myself the chance to tell Landon that my allegiance to the black race does not obviate my embrace of other races, cultures, and histories. I should have told him that in my view any experience of a person who considers himself African American is a black experience and that blackness is not a litmus test one must pass based on pigmentation, phenotype, working class status or a legacy of discrimination. I should have told him that I will never allow my race, gender, class, or sexual orientation to define

What Color Is Your Hoodie?

who I am or limit my artistic aims. But instead of dismantling the wall between the regions of black gay culture we represent, Landon and I piled on more bricks. We missed our opportunity to find harmony in our differences and assuage our mutual anger, longing and frustration.

The Park Bench Promise

Dear Mike—

This letter is long overdue, as most handwritten correspondence is in the hyperconnected digital age we live in where individuals are hyper and anything but connected. Here I go again griping and this is only the start of a very long, earnest missive. Of course you knew that I would complain eventually, that each time I take pen to paper or hammer the keys of my laptop I'm on another rant, trying to illuminate, expose, or provoke. Yet tonight is different; tonight no screeds, no protests. Wearily I have endured the stresses of the day, lasting into the silent, empty hours of morning to give pages and pages of prose to you, my brista.

A funny word, isn't it? Brista: a fusing of the words *brother* and *sister*. The technical term for such a blending is portmanteau. I had never heard of it until quite recently. Have you? Whoever devised it was rather clever I think. Used among black gay men it connotes an enduring bond between gay brothers. Having been raised an only child, I have no idea what it means to experience genuine brotherhood, yet I imagine it isn't all that different from the bond you and I share. Before we were ever bristas we were brothers and even before that we were friends and co-workers. And before that I had no one.

I don't know if you realize what it means to be raised in a family of women like I was. Even though you were surrounded by your sisters growing at least you had your father. A father's love and influence, especially to black boys living in this racist patriarchal society, is unmatched. Even now as you approach middle age your father continues to be a guiding spirit in your life. The men in my family were unconcerned with preparing me for manhood. Fatherless and an only child, surrounded by aunts, female cousins, and their girlfriends, I had to navigate my way to manhood on my own. I didn't even have a close male friend, really. I was a nerd, I was a loner, and I was a fag.

Ironically, I didn't even know I was gay until I went off to college when the sight of a herculean football player virtually naked in the men's bathroom jolted my sex drive in a way stacks of *Playboys* under my grandfather's mattress never could. Still it would be several years—four in fact—before I was comfortable enough with my sexuality to come out to myself, and still a few more years before I learned to love being gay and most of all love myself.

All of that happened around the time I met you. Surely you remember and can never forget. We were both working as assistant managers at Blockbuster Video. You had recently transferred from your store in a suburb of Kansas City, Missouri to my store within the city limits. It was 1994, *Pulp Fiction* and *Forrest Gump* were the biggest films of the year and the war on black men in this country was at a fever pitch. Two years earlier, Rodney King pleaded for Americans to "just get along." Dennis Rodman was acting a fool on and off the basketball court. OJ Simpson had just done to his wife, a white woman, what scores of rappers were doing to women and gay men in their skuzzy lyrics. And in the midst of all this cultural upheaval I had been dismissed from Northwestern University due to poor academic standing. I spent my days working at Blockbuster and my nights watching movies and writing exhaustively in my journal. I didn't go out; I didn't date. No one needed a friend more than I.

I can't recall exactly when you and I began spending time together or under what circumstance. We saw *Pulp Fiction* about four times that summer and laughed at the same jokes each time as if we had never seen the film before. Eventually, when we turned twenty-one—me exactly one day before you—we started going to the casino on Friday nights right after we closed the store. You won $2500 once and I was right there beside you, envious, but still happy for you (and the hundred dollars you gave me). It felt good for the first time in my life to have a guy my own age I could take to, who I could actually call on the phone or go out to dinner with, a guy who was just as much a misfit as I was and who didn't mind all of my quirks.

Perhaps this is why you were the first person I ever came out to. We were dining at a restaurant, and I told you about the short older Italian guy who kept ogling me and smiling at me whenever he came into our store. Remember? The one we secretly laughed at because neither of us could believe a gay guy had a crush on me. Then he asked me out. I said yes, and instead of having a proper date we had sex. You listened to me blubber when he inevitably broke my heart and through it all you never judged, never chastised. Then, about six weeks later, you came out to me. That's when I knew we were brothers.

Bristas came later, when I met the love of my life and relocated with him to Chicago. Long distance relationships can wreak havoc on two people in a romance. For two platonic friends the effort to maintain a strong bond is even more difficult. This all happened in 1999, before Facebook, Twitter, and text messaging, when the culture was on the threshold between paper and paperless, thoughtfully composed letters and egocentric brain farts. As difficult as it was for me to transition into a new environment and a new relationship, I had to recalibrate my relationship with you, a task equally as daunting. We had always shared with each other, confided in each other, come to each other's rescue more times than I can recall. Yet each time I telephoned you during those first two years in Chicago full of frustration and despair you were supportive and encouraging, promising more than once to drive to Chicago in a U-Haul and help me move back to Kansas City if I needed to.

I did the same for you. Like a good friend, I gave you advice and expressed concern when you dated down low married men and openly gay men who simply weren't worthy of the wondrous gifts you have to give. As the years went by you were making a life for yourself, dating, traveling, working hard and playing hard through several relationships, and at the same time my relationship with Gerald solidified. Having a white boyfriend, especially one significantly older than me, always made me feel I was missing out on a valuable experience; that being involved with a black man would somehow give me more connection to my heritage, my culture, and myself. You never once questioned my blackness, as some did. You have always known that I have never preferred one race of men over another, that I enjoy the body of any well-made man regardless of race. When you met Mark I was happy for you. When you told me he lived in Evanston, Illinois, I was overjoyed. Your trips to Chicago and the times you, Mark, Jerry, and I went out together are cherished. It was then I knew you and I had surpassed our bonds as close friends, even brothers. We were bristas.

I thought this letter would be much easier to compose than it is. I thought the words would seep from my pen the same way my poems, stories, and essays seem to liquefy onto the page. Writing is a personal, private enterprise even when the end result is meant for public consumption. But a letter takes care; a letter of this sort takes courage. Don't misunderstand: I don't fear you, my brista, never you. I fear the strength of my feelings for you. Lately I've been reading *Salvation: Black People and Love* by bell hooks. In it she critically assesses the lack of loving relationships between African Americans and the reproduction of destructive relationships among blacks in popular discourse and mass media. I find great truth in hooks' claims. You and I were raised in an era which denied black males access to loving, nurturing relationships with one another. It seems the men of our community were perpetually engaged in warfare, even though this has not always been the case. The streets of every urban area of America have been transformed into channels gushing with the spilled blood of black men. Marlon Riggs' famous quote "Black men loving black men is *the* revolutionary act" couldn't be more accurate. What you, I, and other bristas share is truly a gift. It is a treasure to be guarded jealously, viciously. Harnessed and applied in the right way it could be a potent weapon against all systems of oppression. Imagine.

Andrew Sullivan wrote an entire book on the topic of friendship among gay men, *Love Undetectable: Notes on Friendship, Sex, and Survival,* in which he argues that friendship in some respects is

What Color Is Your Hoodie?

more powerful than familial relationships because individuals must select their friends, unlike family members who they are born with. Friendship demands expression and attention, a common language and tacit agreement. Among black gay men, bristas, friendship relies on unity and acceptance. We share no sexual intimacy. We share no blood ties. Our bond can only be sustained if we empathize with each other and ensure that we maintain safe spaces for one another. This is the core of friendship. Black men, unlike any other group of men, value recognition and identification above all else. I see you; you see me. We nod; we whisper "'Sup?" This is how we belong.

Mike, my friendship with you has been the longest non-familial relationship of my life, and the intimacy I share with you is second only to my intimacy with Jerry. When he and I decided to marry four years ago I picked you to be my best man for all the obvious reasons but also because I knew that more than any other person you would take the commitment seriously. The wedding was much more emotional than I ever thought it would be. For a man who prides himself on being in full possession of his emotions, I nearly passed out at the altar, overcome with breathlessness, sweating, and trembling. And then I felt your hand on my back. You calmed me, gave me a sip of water and told me to breathe. Inhale; accept. Exhale; embrace. You were indeed the best man for the job and continue to support my marriage. I thank you.

Years ago you and I promised we would be old men together sitting on a park bench feeding birds, griping about the state of the world and reminiscing about how great life was when we were younger. I have a head start: I'm already cranky and cynical at this young age. Yet I know you will remain optimistic, loyal, steadfast. I know you will keep our promise to meet me in a place alive with splendor and majesty when the last of our youth had fallen away and we are ready to assume our place as elders of the community. Perhaps by the time we make it to that park bench the world will have replicated the harmony of our friendship, and misfit boys like us will finally be ushered in from the darkness, taken out of the margins and loved; each and every one, brother to brother. This is my greatest wish.

Save a seat for me on that park bench. I'll do the same.
Endure with me,
Jarrett

Real Compared to What?

Though sensitive, the topic of class depictions in black entertainment has been an ongoing debate in the African American community for decades, reaching its apex in the 1980s with the *The Cosby Show*. Popular entertainment straddles a fine line between idealism and reality; in regard to representations of the working, middle, and upper classes of the African American community, the drive to "keep it real" can stifle the creativity of television writers, directors, and producers. *The Cosby Show* and other programs which showcase African Americans who inhabit the middle and upper-class are routinely subjected to negative criticism from black audiences for presenting what they perceive to be apocryphal representations of blacks, claiming these characterizations not only fail to accurately portray the realities of the black majority but conform to an idealized white standard that contributes to cultural genocide. Yet these critics overlook changing economies both within the black community and throughout the nation, not the mention the new educational, political, and social reality African Americans must now grapple with. As diverse as any culture, African Americans exist across a complex socioeconomic spectrum that is constantly broadening and redefining itself, presenting television studios the challenge of keeping pace through radical reinventions of established formats and narratives.

When LOGO, America's first television network devoted to LGBT programming, debuted in 2005, the nation's culture war had reached a stalemate. Several months earlier, same-sex marriage had been trotted out as a wedge issue by Republican Svengali Karl Rove to rally conservative voters to the polls and re-elect George W. Bush. As a counternarrative, popular NBC sitcom *Will & Grace,* concluding after eight seasons, celebrated a cultural milestone by becoming the first network comedy to feature an openly gay character as its lead, and a spate of gay-themed films, most notably *Brokeback Mountain,* were generating revenue at the box office. LOGO's inception capitalized on the zeitgeist by offering LGBT viewers entertainment designed exclusively for them. Among the many offerings on the network was *Noah's Arc,* a black gay incarnation of the common "four-way friendship" structure popularized by sitcoms such as *The Golden Girls, Designing Women,* and *Noah's Arc*'s closest referents, *Sex and the City* and *Girls.* Though it lasted only two seasons with sixteen episodes and an unaired pilot (a feature film, *Noah's Arc: Jumping the Broom,* was released two years after the show's final episode), *Noah's Arc* quickly became LOGO's highest rated scripted series and to date remains the only sitcom in television history to showcase four out black gay men as its central characters. (*The DL Chronicles,* which premiered for one season on here! in 2007, qualifies as an anthology series.) While various topics such as same-sex co-parenting, promiscuity, friendship, and intimacy are prominent themes in the show, class and the way the principle characters represent and commodify class status is perhaps *Noah's Arc*'s most fascinating if not perplexing feature.

    Set in Los Angeles in the mid-2000s, the show chronicles the romantic ups and downs of Noah Nicholson (Darryl Stephens), the show's eponymous lead. As a fledgling screenwriter he represents the creative class and embodies all of the traits of his good friends: university professor Chance (Doug Spearman), HIV educator Alex (Rodney Chester), and boutique owner Ricky (Christian Vincent). The trendy quartet, not unlike the women of *Sex and the City,* environ a fantasy world and remain blissfully unaware of national and international events taking place beyond their comfortable milieu. The sitcom, as if retaliating against the dominant culture for its blindness to the presence of healthy, active black gay men, willfully ignores the dominant white culture, its activities, and preoccupations. Nearly every man the quartet encounters is homosexual, attractive, educated, and financially well off, making

What Color Is Your Hoodie?

plausibility creator, writer, and director Patrik-Ian Polk's greatest weakness. As Gust A. Yep and John P. Elia write, "Although *Noah's Arc* features the lives of four African American gay men who live in South Central Los Angeles—typically characterized as a working-class African American area—the trappings of upper-middle-class American consumerism are omnipresent materially and symbolically in this television series".[5] While the main characters in *Noah's Arc* inhabit the upper- middle class, their personas are clearly meant to appeal to black gay men of all socioeconomic backgrounds. From Noah's wildly eclectic sometimes bizarre fashion choices to Chance's haughty, affected speech patterns and Alex's motherwit, employment of black vernacular and portmanteaux, performance, as much as obvious displays of wherewithal or its lack, indicates to audiences where these characters fit on the socioeconomic ladder. While *Will & Grace* shunned not only working class gays but gay men of color as well (the addition of Taye Diggs as a brief love interest for Will over the course of a four-episode storyline in the show's final season seemed more of an afterthought), Patrik-Ian Polk makes the show appeal to black gay men across a wide socioeconomic landscape, understanding that "[i]t is critical that [*Noah's Arc*] have mass appeal and not be threatening or off-putting to the audience, presumed to be White, middle-class GLBTQ individuals".[6] Not only does the fluid class status of these characters invite the viewership of black gay men from all backgrounds, it relates to middle and upper-class gay white men as well. Yep and Elia claim, "[t]hrough the process of middle-class Whitenization, the characters become familiar and safe to those who are most likely to watch the LOGO Cable Channel".[7] For African American gay men, *Noah's Arc*, like the urban literature of prominent black gay writer E. Lynn Harris, offers aspirational viewers materialism, fantastically gorgeous men, melodrama and a belief that all of it is easily within their grasp.

---

5. Yep, Gust A. and John P. Elia, "Racialized Masculinities and the New Homonormativity in LOGO's *Noah's Arc*." *Journal of Homosexuality* 59, no. 7 (2012): 890-911. http://www.google.scholar.com.
6. Ibid.
7. Ibid.

Although socioeconomic stratifications gird every episode of the series they appear most strikingly in "Nothin' Goin' On but the Rent." This episode, the fourth of the first season, finds the quartet enduring career and financial instability while confronting "ghetto" life in South Central LA. Noah, owing four thousand dollars in back rent, must come to terms with the fact that his writing career, as his new boyfriend Wade (Jensen Atwood) states, is just a hobby until he can earn a living from it, which he does when he finally secures a job rewriting a spec for Paramount Studios, written, ironically, by Wade. Alex quits his job as a counselor at a local clinic to open his own HIV clinic catering to black and Latino men. Ricky's rampant promiscuity allows a shoplifter to abscond with some of his merchandise while he has sex in one of his boutique's dressing rooms. But the most notable class divide can be seen through Chance's newfound friendship with a homothug called T-Money (Catero Colbert) who provides him a crash course in how to act like a thug. Chance's association with T-Money confounds his friends but to calm their anxieties he explains that his interest in T-Money is purely ethnographic and that he is "simply satisfying [his] intellectual curiosity about this [down low], hip-hop phenomenon which seems to have insinuated itself into the hearts and minds of gay black men everywhere".[8] Renamed Lil' C by his mentor T-Money, Chance sips malt liquor from a brown bagged forty-once bottle, sports a bandana wrapped around his head, and makes forced attempts to inflect his ordinarily grammatical speech with gansta slang, all of it to comic effect.

As Chance states, fascination with the down low homothug extends to most black gay men, either as an erotic ideal or merely, as in Chance's case, cultural curiosity. The homothug provides a catalyst to working class ghetto life for the men of *Noah's Arc* as he does to a large swath of professional black gay men. Both a social rebel and a sexual outlaw, the homothug symbolizes the class schism among African American gay men in the twenty-first century. Keith Boykin argues that:

---

8. *Noah's Arc*. "Nothin' Goin' On but the Rent". Episode no. 5 first broadcast on 9 Nov. 2005 by LOGO. Written and directed by Patrik-Ian Polk.

What Color Is Your Hoodie?

The marriage of hip hop and homosexuality has created a divide in the black community with surprising new fault lines. The new divide is not so much between black homosexuals and heterosexuals as it is among black homosexuals themselves, split along generational, political, and social boundaries.[9]

Typically dressed in an oversized T-shirt, sagging jeans that partially expose his buttocks, and work boots, the homothug bears all the monikers of "the hood," embodying unqualified masculinity, criminality, danger, and desire. He offers many black gay men a lustful fantasy tinged with his rebellious nature and brash lack of decorum, yet he problematizes identity politics for the central characters of *Noah's Arc*.

Although *Noah's Arc* makes no pointed class critique (the double meaning of the show's title makes it plane that everyone black and gay will be included in both the main character's and the sitcom's arc) it is clear that the working class, in the characters' estimation, should be kept in its place. Of the members of the quartet, Chance has the least engagement with the working class. Pretentious, uptight, and judgmental, Chance separated from his new live-in boyfriend Eddie (Jonathan Julian) in the previous episode, "Don't Mess with My Man," after catching him cheating with a man on the down low. Upon this discovery the quartet, along with Wade and Alex's muscle-bound hypermasculine partner Trey (Gregory Keith) in the mix, file into Chance's luxury SUV and motor to the ghetto to catch Eddie in the act. When Chance literally drives his expensive SUV into the home of Eddie's paramour, this action communicates the black gay middle class's refusal to be brought down by the machinations of black gay men of the working class, whether out or closeted. The middle class comforts they enjoy can only be preserved through the exclusion of the working class. Upon taking up with T-Money, Chance, outfitted in thug attire and not the slacks and argyle sweaters he customarily wears, has an argument with Eddie over Chance spending time with T-Money while he babysits Eddie's daughter Kenya. Chance slaps Eddie then,

---

9. Boykin, Keith. *Beyond the Down Low: Sex, Lies, and Denial in Black America.* (New York: Carroll & Graf Publishers, 2005), 234.

both of them now aroused, they embrace and kiss lustily, reunited at last. It is only then, after T-Money has reignited his and Eddie's sexual desire that Chance terminates his friendship with T-Money. The homothug is given merely erotic power within the context of Chance and Eddie's relationship and indeed within the ethos of the milieu they inhabit. T-Money, despite expressing an interest in art house cinema and other upper-class pursuits, can never be a worthy suitor for Chance so long as he remains a thug and a threat to black gay domesticity.

As representatives of what journalist Eugene Robinson terms the black Mainstream, the men of *Noah's Arc*, "cluster together in [a] black majority enclave, [not] out of necessity but out of choice".[10] Racial pride, solidarity, and the desire for racial uplift, as demonstrated by the volunteer work the quartet performs throughout the series, particularly at Alex's clinic, indicates their commitment to the race, yet "[a] shift in class values occurs in black life when integration comes and with it the idea that money is the primary marker of individual success, not how one acquires it."[11] The gallery of men who orbit Noah and his cohort can only remain in their peer group by meeting select criteria: they must be out of the closet, proud of their homosexuality, upwardly mobile and committed to fighting HIV/AIDS. These are noble qualities and, one could argue, the thesis of the entire series. Even when Noah and Wade experience financial instability they retain their place in the milieu because they are strivers and committed to protecting and uplifting the black gay community, not imperiling it like down low men.

Wade, Noah's love interest, presents the most complex rendering of class on the show. Though he was raised in privilege, superficial yet contradictory class markers—his hair styled in cornrolls, his luxury condo, employment as a screenwriter in season one and his job during season two as a furniture delivery man—enhance

---

10. Robinson, Eugene. *Disintegration: The Splintering of Black America*. (New York: Anchor Books, 2010), 194.
11. hooks, bell. *We Real Cool: Black Men and Masculinity*. (New York: Routledge, 2004), 18.

What Color Is Your Hoodie?

his appeal as a hybridized black gay man, possessing not only fluid sexuality (at the start of the series Wade identified as heterosexual) but fluid class status as well. Though Noah cheats on Wade in season one, an action which terminated their relationship, by the season two finale the star-crossed pair reunite. Yet by this point time in the story's arc their fortunes have switched: Noah is now the successful screenwriter and Wade is forced to earn a living as a delivery man. As the show's romantic hero, Wade, like the sitcom itself, must amalgamate a host of masculine roles and identities: at alternate moments he is Noah's friend, lover, scold, collaborator, rival, enemy, and critic. The ambivalence Noah expresses about his relationship with Wade in season one dissipates in the second season once Wade is comfortably involved with another man and brought down to a lower economic level, yet as evidenced by the pair's lavish wedding in the feature film *Noah's Arc: Jumping the Broom*, Wade does not remain in impecunious circumstances for long. Wade's family resides in Orange County, one of the wealthiest areas in the nation, and owns a home in Martha's Vineyard where he and Noah eventually wed.

Noah's Arc is a black-themed sitcom that, refreshingly, never deals with racism. Encounters with Caucasian characters are kept to a minimum, allowing issues of homophobia, effemiphobia, masculinity, fidelity, individualism, and class to manifest within each and every relationship. The true antagonist of the series, however, is down low behavior. Coming at the height of the cultural dialogue surrounding the DL (brought into the zeitgeist by author J.L. King's book *On the Down Low*, and his subsequent appearance on *The Oprah Winfrey Show*, as well as Keith Boykin's nonfiction book on the same topic), closeted black men are looked upon with palpable derision by the quartet of *Noah's Arc*, and of the four couples on the show (Chance and Eddie, Noah and Wade, Alex and Trey, Ricky and Junito (Wilson Cruz)) three are threatened by men on the down low. Eddie's infidelity with a down low man provided a story arc in season one that had implications for many of the other characters. In season two, Guy, a straight-identified houseguest who becomes sexually obsessed with Alex's Adonis partner Trey nearly succeeds in sabotaging their relationship. Wade and Noah, edging toward reconciliation after their break up in the season one finale, find their situation complicated by Baby Gat (Jason Steed), a down low English rapper. *Noah's Arc's* stance on unsafe sex and the characters' commitment to preventing the spread of HIV/AIDS through their volunteer work at Alex's clinic inform viewers that "behavior, not [black men's] identity . . . creates the conditions for the spread of HIV."[12] Whether men on the DL are working class like Eddie's trick or wealthy celebrities like Baby Gat, this behavior not only threatens the individuals involved and poses danger to the entire community, it reinforces stereotypes white people have that black men are hypersexual beings and simultaneously reinforces the same stereotypes many African Americans have of gay men.[13] In the show's complex ethos, down low behavior is synonymous with a working class pathology regardless of the socioeconomic status of the man who practices it because the out black gay community Noah and his friends represent possess the education, money, and support system—not to mention integrity and pride in their sexuality—to fortify themselves against such behaviors. Layli Phillips links down low discourse and poverty by explaining that such dialogue prevents urgent cultural conversations surrounding poverty and HIV/AIDS from taking place. She writes:

Poverty is correlated with a host of other factors, from race, to needle-sharing, to lack of access to barriers for safer sex, to lack of access to appropriate medical care, even prevention and intervention. Thus, the "down low" discourse is a diversion from this important yet politically controversial fact.[14]

Even in spite of their professional and economic success, Baby Gat and Guy, given the show's arrangements, are considered working class by the quartet because they refuse to be honest

---

12. Boykin, Keith. *Beyond the Down Low: Sex, Lies, and Denial in Black America.* (New York: Carroll & Graf Publishers, 2005), 158.
13. Ibid 151.
14. Phillips, Layla. "Deconstructing 'Down Low' Discourse: The Politics of Sexuality, Gender, Race, AIDS, and Anxiety". *Journal of African American Studies* 9 no. 2: (2005) 3-15 http://www.google.scholar.com.

about their sexual identity and perpetuate self-destructive behavior, blaming those around them for their failures in love rather than own and acknowledge their culpability.

Guy (Benjamin Patterson) presents the biggest threat of the down low to the black gay middle class. As Alex and Trey's houseguest during season two, he was initially introduced to the quartet as a close friend of Wade and represented himself as solidly heterosexual. Yet Alex suspects from the beginning that Guy has a sexual interest in Trey, an accusation no one in the series believes until Guy begins to show psychotic tendencies by cutting himself with a butcher knife and forging Alex's name on a suicide note. As an HIV educator, Alex accurately recognizes Guy as the threat he is, not just to his domestic life but to the health and welfare of the black gay community, itself a microcosm of the entire African American community. Once the truth is revealed and Trey evicts him from his and Alex's home, not only is the rift in their relationship repaired but the final threat to the quartet is eliminated. In the following episode they all participate in the Ovahness Ball, a charity event which takes place over Black Gay Pride Weekend in Los Angeles. It is here that the series comes to its abrupt conclusion, with all couples reunited, and Wade and his current partner Dre (Merwin Mondesir), a bartender, victims of a car crash. Though Wade survives and goes on to marry Noah in the feature film, viewers never learn Dre's fate.

Like most television programs, gay-themed sitcoms rarely examine the lives of individuals who live below the poverty line or just above it. The poor and working class are customarily characterized as pathologically self-destructive, unmotivated, uneducated, and amoral. In the years since *Noah's Arc* aired its final episode, few gay characters of color have populated the television landscape; most notable exceptions include characters in *Looking, True Blood*, and *DTLA*. Although racial and ethnic diversity remains a point of contention among many viewers, fair and honest representations of socioeconomic diversity also present problems for television studios. Though few can deny the on-going rise of African Americans into the upper-class, poor blacks of all identities and orientations find their portrayals limited, a wide gulf from the working class black-themed sitcoms of the 1970s which included *Sanford and Son* and *Good Times*. Although *Noah's Arc* embodied many flaws, it must nevertheless be celebrated for giving visibility to a population of the LGBT community that so often gets ignored in popular entertainment.

Bibliography

Boykin, Keith. *Beyond the Down Low: Sex, Lies, and Denial in Black America*. (New York: Carroll & Graf Publishers, 2005).

hooks, bell. *We Real Cool: Black Men and Masculinity*. (New York: Routledge, 2004).

Noah's Arc. "Nothin' Goin' On but the Rent". Episode no. 5 first broadcast on 9 Nov. 2005 by LOGO. Written and directed by Patrik-Ian Polk.

Phillips, Layla. "Deconstructing 'Down Low' Discourse: The Politics of Sexuality, Gender, Race, AIDS, and Anxiety". *Journal of African American Studies* 9 no. 2: (2005) 3-15 http://www.google.scholar.com.

Robinson, Eugene. *Disintegration: The Splintering of Black America*. (New York: Anchor Books, 2010), 194.

Yep, Gust A. and John P. Elia, "Racialized Masculinities and the New Homonormativity in LOGO's *Noah's Arc*." *Journal of Homosexuality* 59, no. 7 (2012): 890-911. http://www.google.scholar.com.

Sam I Am

At thirty-four years old I decided to learn how to play football. The idea came about from an encounter I had with a bear I encountered at the Market Days street festival in August. A wide, big-boned man with a beer keg belly dressed in cargo shorts and a lime green hoodie, he bounded up to me on the street, looked me up and down and without saying a word cradled me in his arms and hoisted me above his head. The entire festival tilted in my eyes but before I had the chance to object he put me back on my feet and announced that I was going to play football, no excuses, no objections. "We need your muscles on the field," he said. Initially, I laughed him off, dismissing him as just another out-to-lunch white man who thought my blackness alone qualified me as a stellar athlete. But the more I thought about it the more I wanted the chance to quash the fear and disdain I associated with football. So I signed up with the Chicago Metropolitan Sports Association a few days later and was assigned to one of its recreational gay teams.

The Drake Demons were a great group of guys: about a dozen men in their thirties and forties who each had his own unique experience with football. Some of my teammates were diehard football fans nostalgic for the days they played football in high school. They wanted to recapture the fun and folly of their youth without the hypermacho competitiveness and trash talk associated with guys in the competitive gay football league (those gargantuan alpha-males obliterated any stereotypes of gay men being effeminate sissies who were clueless at sports; they played to win and commonly sent their competitors to the hospital). My other teammates were novices like me who confessed to feeling something akin to PTSD being on the football field. We had each been traumatized by our peers, maniacal coaches, or red-faced dads who cussed at us from the sidelines when we had played the sport in our childhood; none of us ever quite recovered from it. We scrubs knew next to nothing about sports, and even among our gay brethren we felt out of place. I will never forget seeing teammates who were accomplished lawyers, physicians, and bankers in their everyday life crumple into self-consciousness once the opposing team arrived and the game began. Two of them never returned after the first game.

I have never been a sports fan. Perhaps I never shall be. It all looks so intimidating, this business of running, throwing, and catching; massive bodies crashing into one another; the snap of bones and gush of blood. Few healthy, able-bodied men escape boyhood without being pulled into the vortex of sports, and most boys love it. How else to occupy and exhaust tots with too much energy and teens who have no outlet for the natural aggression testosterone pumps into their developing bodies. Yet for the boys like me—the nerds, sissies, outcasts, and uncoordinated buffoons who warm the bench and shuffle through gym class with our heads hanging down—participation in sports is punitive, and it can be painful. There is no fear quite like the fear of being the last player picked for a team, no pain as sharp as the billion needles that prick every part of your body when you accept the fact that you don't measure up and you will never fit in. For a boy whose entire male world consisted of over-muscled cartoon characters and an alcoholic grandfather who plain didn't give a damn, being called a scrubby faggot in gym class was worse violence than any beat down I ever got.

I've never been one to put stock in conspiracy theories, but I sometimes think football was a game designed by straight guys to keep women and gay men away from them for a few hours each week. It appears, to an outsider like me, to be a determinedly complicated sport, not unlike a Rube Goldberg machine. Accounting for yards, learning a new vocabulary (I still don't know what a scrimmage is or the difference between sacking and tackling), and comprehending the various line formations, for me, would take more time than I

What Color Is Your Hoodie?

would ever want to devote to a sport. Unlike baseball and basketball, sports with explicit goals (hit a small white ball and run around four bases; shoot a big orange ball through a hoop) no aspect of football appears to be as simple as it could be. From my novice's perspective the whole game is needlessly complex, laden with contrivances that serve no purpose but to obfuscate players and spectators alike. It takes a combined group effort to power a football team to victory and I am much too individualistic for that. I usually feel I alone am to blame if our team loses yet very little pride in collective victory. To this day I can't recall how many games the Drake Demons won or lost while I was a teammate. But in football the win and only the win is what counts. No one cares how it came about. Advancing the aims of the team is much more important than the contributions, or lack of contributions, of the individual. This is the social ethic of all sports, the tacitly understood moto players and fans alike adhere to.

As the rest of the culture shifts its social consciousness toward a greater acceptance of feminism and homosexuals, and the collected voices of the subaltern rally for an end to white patriarchal dominance and its multitudinous expressions, football has become the last bastion for traditional American manhood. No other area of American society, with the possible exception of the military, cordons off a space for men to exhibit a brand of masculinity so primal and destructive anyone who exists outside of its boundaries becomes vulnerable to its grizzly abuses. Criminal cases involving dog fighting (Michael Vick), pedophilia (Jerry Sandusky), violence against women (Ray Rice) and children (Adrian Peterson), and murder-suicide (Jovan Belcher) has transformed football into the nation's shame. Criticism of football, which has ostensibly replaced baseball as America's pastime, has grown louder and more charged in recent years, with even President Obama stating that if he had a son he wouldn't allow him to play the game. The long term risk to players' health, the outrageous salaries college football coaches receive (a staggering eight figures at some institutions) and the ethos which exhorts all participants to win at all costs has lowered the prestige of this game to depths from which it may never rebound.

Then came Michael Sam. A formidable stack of granite muscle, Sam, a quarterback from the University of Missouri—Columbia—the state I was born and raised in—Sam fought his way out of abject poverty in rural Texas to become one of the nation's top athletes. Endowed with chestnut skin and wide set eyes, mountainous shoulders, and the thickest thighs and ass I've ever glimpsed on a man, Michael Sam is no one you'd ever want to piss off. Ever. He has come to emblemize, in heroic fashion, all that I wished for myself when I came out as gay man: physical beauty, virility, power, wit, intelligence, and bold masculinity. He, like Jason Collins and other out gay athletes, holds an enviable place within the gay community because he can do what few of us can: successfully navigate America's most rigidly masculine environment, fraught with homophobia, without qualifying or compromising his gay identity or his black identity. His choice to live his life openly and with pride strikes a salvo at an American institution that has garnered ignominious publicity in recent years. Within the swirl of such ignoble acts, Michael Sam's coming out story can be seen as both football's saving grace and the symbol for its strides to embrace equality. Through Sam, football has the opportunity to redeem itself, to shatter one of its longstanding prejudices and, by doing so, atone for the damage it has done to countless individuals and rebrand itself.

ESPN couldn't leave him alone after he came out. Day after day there were reports, roundtable discussions between the talking heads, opinion polls, and postings on social media. What will coming out do to Michael Sam's chances of getting drafted? What will it be like, the talking heads pontificated, to have an openly gay man in the locker room with all the other players? Each time I went to the gym I felt a sense of triumph surge within me when I saw Michael Sam displayed on every flatscreen in the gym. It was like a member of my family suddenly becoming famous. I wanted to stop people in the middle of their workout, point to the flatscreen and say, "I know him." And even though I've never met Michael Sam I know him in the sense that we share the same story: black gay men living in a society doing everything it can to eradicate us. But it can't.

What Color Is Your Hoodie?

Whether he likes it or not, Michael Sam has come to symbolize the nation's dual overarching social ideologies: the conservative masculinist ethos which expresses itself through violence, competition, domination, and anti-intellectualism and the liberal multicultural *raison d' être* which champions a revisionist model of masculinity that abolishes macho puffery, chauvinism, homophobia, racism, and violence. Though to the dominate culture black gay men have always existed on the periphery of society and were only seen when we were prancing around in drag or dying of AIDS, Michael Sam, like Jason Collins, forces American culture and football culture to reckon with its own racism and homophobia by introducing them the thing they fear most: an openly gay black man who is not only unimpeachably masculine—a strike against their stereotypical notions about effeminacy in gay men—but frank about his desire for white men. Without question, Michael Sam has changed the conversation about black gay men and masculinity.

This, is essence, is what it all boils down to—masculinity. Patriarchal manhood views any expressions of love and tenderness as weakness. The worst thing for a black man is to appear weak, especially in the presence of white society. Eldridge Cleaver's venomous comments about black gay men come roaring back: "The white man has deprived him [black gay men] of his masculinity, castrated him in the center of his burning skull, and when he . . . takes the white man for his lover". The image of Michael Sam passionately kissing a white man, his partner Vito Cammisano, or the idea of the two of them having sex upends stereotypes about black men, gay men, and football players. The unmooring of black and gay stereotypes and the reductive dichotomous relationships connected to them has left the dominate culture scrambling to reclaim a vision of American masculinity that resists critique and alteration.

Out of 256 draft picks Michael Sam, a first team All-American player, was selected 249 in the seventh and final round of the draft. The NFL draft takes several days, and while the nation's favorite sport hemmed and hawed and took their sweet time making up their minds whether or not they should allow an out and proud gay man into their locker rooms and onto their Astroturf, Michael and Vito holed up in Michael's agent's home riding a veritable roller coaster that plunged the powerhouse athlete into catatonia then surged him into a paroxysm of tears when, at last, he received the call from the St. Louis Rams that they had drafted him, the entire ordeal videotaped for a documentary that aired months later on OWN. The image of him in *Out Magazine* staring directly at me, steely-eyed and unflappable, ready to storm onto a football field, and at the same time vulnerable like a newly hatched starling reluctant to spread his wings, the word Truth written in chalky white letters across his chest as if to shield him. He is out there, amid the rumpus and the spotlight of celebrity, pursued and derided, chatted up and rumored about, but he is not alone.

Aside from being black, gay, and romantically involved with white men, Michael Sam and I have very little in common. I'm a big man but he's bigger. He's younger. I'm more educated. My usual attire is a cardigan and a tie. He goes through most days dressed in workout gear and athletic shoes. We're both committed to working out, yet I loathe cardio, always have, and have to force myself onto the treadmill each time I visit the gym. But not Michael. He's a runner and a thousand times better at it than I'll ever be. But whenever I step onto the treadmill's unforgiving black conveyor, I press Quick Start, crank up the pace, close my eyes, surrender my body to the velocity and rigor of the run, and suddenly I am Michael Sam, a juggernaut of muscle, stamina and coordination. My breathing labors and my heels nearly kick the small of my back as I sprint down my imagined football field hearing only cheers and the cherished beat of my own heart.

Peewee's Peepee

When I was nine years-old my aunt Retha Mae and her husband Ronnie took me on vacation with them to Disneyworld. My mother, twenty-three at the time, was working a string of low paying jobs to support me and pay her share of rent for an apartment she shared with a close girlfriend. Women like my mother who give birth as teenagers need all the help and support they can get, not only to boost their confidence and encourage them to complete their education and strive for success, but also to provide their children with material comforts they cannot. Mama was happy her sister and brother-in-law were being so generous and could give me the kind of splashy summer vacation she longed to but simply couldn't afford. My aunt, ever scrupulous, had an ulterior motive in mind when she included me in her family's vacation plans. She saw the trip not only as a fun-filled excursion for me and her daughter, my six-year-old cousin Refoni, but also a chance to connect with my grandfather's relatives in Tallahassee and learn about our family's past. As large as my family was, we never spent any time with my grandfather's relatives, and they were seldom discussed. This fracture in our family network pained my aunt, who served as our family historian. Retha Mae wanted to establish bonds with our country kin. So a few days after we arrived in Orlando, my uncle rented a car and the four of us drove two hundred and fifty-six miles to the Panhandle.

The Neals lived in five blue and green ramshackle one-story homes on an isolated spread of flat, dusty land several miles outside of Tallahassee. Decades earlier, like so many other African American families in the South, they had earned their living as cotton pickers and tenant farmers until various economic, agricultural, and technological changes rendered their services obsolete. Enterprising blacks like my grandparents migrated to cities in the North and West. Others stayed behind and made the best of a bad situation. Upon our arrival, my family and I were introduced to packs of people we had never heard of before, yet they all seemed to know me and my cousin and the major aspects of our lives and went to great pains to make us city slickers feel welcome. We were, after all, family.

One of the women, who introduced herself as my grandfather's niece, hugged me tight, squeezed my cheeks and waved her sons over to come greet me. Immediately, three little boys, all barefoot, came sprinting toward me, kicking up sepia clouds of dust and dirt with each step. We were all around the same age, yet as a sheltered only child my only playmates were my cousins, who were all girls. Playtime with boys was something I longed for yet feared. I was more inclined to read or play with action figures than rough house, and these country cousins of mine had been reared in an environment that encouraged little boys to be as rowdy as they wished. My mother's other sisters, aunts less tactful than Retha Mae, would have called them rugrats who needed a good ass whooping. Despite my trepidation, all four of us tore off into the hot, sticky night, running, jumping, and wrestling throughout the area while Refoni played dolls with the little girls and my aunt and uncle better acquainted themselves with our distant relations.

After a couple hours of horseplay, the boys' mother found us sweaty and covered in dust and made all of us go to her home and take a bath. D'Juan, who was a year older than me, turned on the hot water, tossed in a bar of Ivory Soap, and instructed all of us to undress and get in. I watched him and his brothers peel off their dusty clothes and leap into the hot bath; they splashed each other gleefully and pitched balled up soggy white washcloths and the bar of soap back and forth, the soap now dingy from the dirt of their bodies. Clearly bathing together was a common practice for them and they beckoned me to remove my clothes and join them. Apprehensive, I slowly unlaced my sneakers and took them off one by one along with my socks. Next, I removed my Pac Man

What Color Is Your Hoodie?

T-shirt and the brand new denim shorts my mother had purchased for me at Jones Department Store where she worked part-time as a salesgirl. I was down to my tighty-whiteys when D'Juan, whose voice at ten was already deep and commanding, said, "What you waiting for? C'mon in."

When I pulled down my briefs the boys stopped their horseplay, pointed at my penis and laughed. "What's wrong with your thing?" D'Juan said.

When I looked down I saw nothing strange, certainly nothing that would inspire the cackling these boys, my distant relatives, broke in to. While it was obvious they weren't surprised to see another boy's genitals, I soon realized that unlike their penises, which looked like charred shrimp, the head of my penis was hooded beneath a layer of skin. Seeing it through their eyes, it reminded me of a miniature elephant's trunk.

* * *

I lie to the nurse and tell her I came to see the doctor because of a sore throat. When she leaves and Dr. O'Connor enters the examination room I'm still reluctant to tell him the real reason I'm here. But when I admit that I fabricated symptoms because I was too embarrassed to talk to a stranger about something so private, especially a woman, concern illuminates his face like a white headlight on a dark stretch of highway and makes me feel guilty.

"I think I need to be circumcised."

After this admission, the doctor fills the space between us with a litany of questions: Are you experiencing any pain? Does your urine flow in a stream or does it spray? When you pull back the foreskin can you see the head of your penis?

"I can't pull the foreskin back at all."

Dr. O'Connor sits down on a small red stool in front of me and sets his clipboard on the lid of a silver trash can. He folds his arms. He exhales. He raises an eyebrow. "You've never seen the head of your penis?"

"No."

"Not even when you have sex?"

I grip the examination table. "I-I've never had sex."

The doctor scratches the back of his head and looks down at his chart, appearing to search for an answer to a question I have not asked. "Do you masturbate?"

"Well . . . yes."

"And you don't see the head then?"

I shake my head and glance at his brown brogues.

Dr. O'Connor stands and reaches across the counter for a pair of cream colored vinyl gloves he removes from a blue and white cardboard box. "Drop your pants. Let me see."

Dr. O'Connor is burly, possessing the solidly built physique of a man who once barreled through life exhibiting unmatched strength, power and force. I can easily picture him forty years earlier tackling men on a football field or strangling them with his bare hands in the jungles of Vietnam. His body sags and his face hangs loose with wrinkles. His hands tremble a bit and his eyebrows are two unruly thatches of white hair, yet he still exudes hypermasculinity and a drill sergeant's gruffness that imposes and intimidates. No doubt Dr. O'Connor was a handsome man in his youth; he still retains some of the rugged, square-jawed appeal of a classic Hollywood star. Like Spencer Tracy, Gary Cooper or John Wayne, his masculinity asserts itself in the bass of his voice and each controlled movement of his body. As I fumble with my belt buckle I wonder what this old white man must be thinking about me, what judgments, if any, he is making about me, a young man who obviously harbors a great deal of shame about his body.

And I do. When I was a toddler and my mother bathed me she would tap the back of my hand whenever I touched my penis. This action had consequences. For years I never even washed my genitals, believing they were shameful and bad. I never retracted my foreskin to urinate, not only because I feared my body and its functions but also because my mother, who was fourteen when I was born, was unaware herself that I was supposed to pull it back. She was raised in a family of women just as I was, and such discussions did not take place. We knew no other way.

What Color Is Your Hoodie?

With my pants and underwear bunched at my ankles, Dr. O'Connor squats before me, lifts my flaccid penis and circles the glans with the tip of the index finger of his other hand. My throat closes as the doctor applies his vinyl-gloved hands. His touch is clinical and benign, as passionless as a plumber's calloused palm on a cold leaky faucet, yet it is the first foreign touch my penis has known since infancy, and I struggle against my body and my emerging homosexuality, determined to not to respond to the sensation. My entire body warms with the yearning to be sexually desirable and from the embarrassment I feel of somehow being damaged, malformed, grotesque. Yet this is one of the reasons I have sought the doctor's medical opinion. He knows bodies; surely he will help introduce me to my own. I look down and watch his bushy white eyebrows crinkle and relax as he inspects my penis. He places the head between his thumb and forefinger and begins to retract the foreskin carefully. Yet despite the gentleness of his hands pain announces itself, a searing pain that intensifies as the foreskin gradually retracts. I wince, grit my teeth and stomp a foot, but Dr. O'Connor doesn't stop until the glans appears, and for the first time in my life I see the head of my penis.

Dr. O'Connor grunts and rises. "You'll see Dr. Elkins." His gloves come off with an ear-splitting snap; he balls them into his fist. He snatches his clipboard, pitches the gloves into the trash can and hastily scribbles with an annoyed look on his face. "He'll straighten you out."

* * *

Phimosis.

To me the word sounds like an exotic cheese. Perhaps this is because of the smegma I imagine has accumulated beneath the foreskin from lack of retraction and proper cleaning.

Dr. Elkins, my urologist, says that circumcision is the best and only option to correct my condition. He schedules a date for the surgery and hands me a small packet of literature: two pamphlets (one describes the procedure, the other details safe sex practices), hospital liability and insurance forms.

For the next three weeks I am the subject of intense conversation among the women in my family. Though none of them is bold enough to approach me and ask about the procedure directly, my cousin Alexis, Lexy as we call her, keeps me apprised of their concerns. *Is Peewee going to be all right? It won't hurt him, will it? He'll be able to have babies, won't he?* I know they are genuinely concerned about my health and welfare, but their inquiries, despite being conducted behind my back, make me feel like a carnival attraction, the Bearded Lady or the Snake-Man. Of my mother's seven siblings only two are men, and the family lost them to alcoholism, drug use, vice, and various stints in prison. When he was alive, my grandfather limited his presence in our lives to brief moments of sobriety, episodes of congeniality markedly different from the raging bull he became when he was drunk. My world is a world of women, and through them I learn of the many health concerns that plague women. They keep no secrets from each other and make me privy to every conversation regarding maladies as far ranging as urinary tract infections, breast self-examinations, and pre-menstrual cramps. They want to know about circumcision for their own education as much as their concern over me. I am the "good man" in the family, the man who must replace their father and brothers. I walked my mother down the aisle when she married my stepfather. Years from now I will do the same for my aunt Faye. They are all invested in me.

* * *

I've heard stories: infant boys whose penises were maimed or burned off during a botched circumcision, forced to undergo gender reassignment. The most startling of these stories concerns David Reimer who, after living the first fifteen years of his life as a girl, learned of the accident that occurred during his own circumcision and his parents' wrenching decision to alter his body forever. After this discovery he began living as a male only to experience incomprehensible emotional and psychological strife and, sadly,

What Color Is Your Hoodie?

committed suicide at thirty-eight years old. In another story an elderly man who checked into the hospital for a routine prostate examination had his penis removed by mistake when his physician misdiagnosed him with penile cancer. Scorned wife Lorena Bobbitt took a cleaver, chopped off cheating husband John Bobbitt's penis in his sleep and tossed it into the gutter as she sped down the street in her car. Soldiers going to war fear their genitals may be mutilated or destroyed in the line of duty, and some of them freeze their sperm so that they can still father children if a tragic event befalls them. Credible threats. Cautionary tales. Horror stories.

* * *

Dr. Elkins told me to wear boxer shorts, and I do. Three days ago, on my day off from Blockbuster Video, I went to the Gap and bought a pair of gold paisley boxers to wear especially for the surgery. I own over a dozen pair of boxer shorts, so my motives for purchasing a new pair are unclear to me. Perhaps I want to show off for the nurses. The old caveat of being sure to wear clean underwear in case you get into an accident comes to mind, which makes me think of "A Good Man Is Hard to Find," Flannery O'Connor's brilliant short story I read in my freshman composition class when I briefly attended Rockhurst College after academic dismissal from Northwestern. Upon my first reading I shuddered at the story's violent ending and couldn't get the grandmother out of my mind for weeks after our class discussed it. Like her I suppose I want to be properly attired if my operation goes awry. This is the first surgical procedure I've ever had. It is 1994. I am twenty years old.

I wake at five thirty in the morning, shower and groom. I cannot eat or drink any fluid other than water. My stomach growls incessantly. After my shower I put on my new boxers; over them I wear a pair of loose gym shorts. Then I put on a T-shirt, socks, Nikes, and go sit in the living room to wait for my mother to arrive.

Granny, still in her nightgown, sits in her favorite chair opposite the television and sips coffee. Since Granddaddy died three years ago she has no reason to be awake so early in the morning. Yet she would never let me leave without seeing me off. She would accompany my mother and me to the surgical center if I asked her, but I want her to stay behind and rest. When I return from the clinic, she will have a hot meal ready for me whether I want it or not.

"You ain't scared, are you?" she asks.

I tell her I am not afraid. I am anxious for the operation to be over, anxious to recover and be made whole once again, but I do not communicate these thoughts to her. I scribble them in my journal along with innumerable thoughts, fears, hopes, desires. Life has given Granny enough worry and misery. I only want to give her love.

My mother arrives late. She is usually late. Luckily we don't have far to go and the roads will be relatively clear. Though it is only mid-May the temperature, even at this early hour of morning, is above normal, the air muggy. I would drive myself but I am not allowed to. I will be under anesthesia during the operation, both general and local, and after the operation, once the anesthesia wears off, I will be in pain. "You'll sleep for a long time after," Dr. Elkins told me in our last consultation before the surgery. "Sex, any kind of sex, will be out of the question for a few weeks." He winked at me.

Sex will be out of the question for much longer than a few weeks.

Dressed in oversized sweatpants and one of her husband's white T-shirts, Mama's face is as sleep drawn and puffy as Granny's. This is far from the way she normally looks. This morning she is not the fashionista I grew up with, the model and fitness enthusiast who relatives joke about putting on make-up before she goes outside to collect the mail, the light-skinned cheerleader turned teenaged mother who maintains a disciplined body and still exudes confidence. She doesn't say much as she drives but when she does her tone is calm and reassuring. "Everybody's been worried," she says with a quarter-smile, "but I told them not to be. You know your aunts."

"I'm surprised they didn't ask for pictures."

She tells me to hush then chuckles with conspiratorial delight. Since she gave birth to me when she was just a teenager, my mother

What Color Is Your Hoodie?

and I have always had a close relationship, at times more akin to big sister-little brother than mother and son. For years I have been her ride along buddy, her sidekick and occasionally her confidant, yet as I sit beside her now I cannot imagine what thoughts are formulating in her mind. Despite our closeness, sex is a topic that has never been on the table for us. The knowledge I gained about puberty and sex I acquired from a special program in sixth grade sponsored by Proctor and Gamble along with watching countless hours of pornography when I matured, including the glossy hardcore porn magazines Granddaddy stashed beneath the mattress of his and Granny's bed. Even when I told her I was getting circumcised she asked no questions about my health or my sex life. Her questions concerning insurance and recuperation have substituted for those directly related to my penis, sex, and self-esteem. Yet not long after my circumcision she will stop calling me Peewee and begin calling me Jarrett.

Once we arrive at the surgical center a nurse points Mama to the waiting room and escorts me to a room in back where I fill out paperwork, undress, lock my clothes in a closet, and put on a thin cotton hospital gown. Short and flimsy, it is soft against my skin and stark white. When I come out of the room the same nurse leads me to a large open area suffused with natural light where other patients repose on gurneys while nurses in sneakers and pastel blue scrubs prep them for various surgical procedures. I lie down on a gurney and my nurse inserts an IV into a vein on the back of my hand and places a bandage over it. I am surprised that the needle doesn't hurt and begin to imagine the operation, the instruments Dr. Elkins will use to separate my foreskin from my penis, how it will look once the operation is over, how I will come to know my body again. The prep area is restful and silent save for intermittent clicks, dings, and whirrs from apparatuses tethered to drowsy patients and the sound of nurses and physicians softly padding back and forth across the space. A slight chill in the air offers relief from the heat outdoors. A gentle classical tune, which I will one day recognize as Debussy's "Clair De Lune", lilts from speakers secreted in the walls and ceiling. All this combined with the seductive slipperiness of the hospital gown against my naked prone body lulls me into somnolence. I begin to get an erection but quickly rouse myself and turn my thoughts to other concerns so my penis will become flaccid again.

In the operating room, with Dr. Elkins and two nurses making final surgical preparations on either side of me, I envision D'Juan and his brothers laughing and pointing at my penis and experience the same heavy feeling of shame I did all those years ago in that pokey bathroom of his mother's home in a cowtown outside of Tallahassee. I see myself at twelve years old in a locked public bathroom stall standing in front of the toilet with my knees bent and my pelvis tilted forward so my urine won't splash my clothes. I see myself at thirteen learning to masturbate in my bedroom, realizing that I shouldn't stroke my penis too vigorously or else it will hurt. I see myself in the men's locker room of Patton Gym at Northwestern wrapping a towel around my waist before I pull down my shorts, pretending to fold my clothes when I'm really waiting for the other men to leave the communal showers so they will not see my uncut dick, flat chest, bony arms, and other inadequate parts. I see the cocks of all the men in every porn video or magazine I've ever seen—oversized, potent, blunt, hypermasculine. I see myself as I am: prone, nearly naked, young and underweight, fearful of no one as much as myself.

Dr. Elkins, masked so that only his rascally blue eyes are visible, says, "Okay, Jarrett, we're ready? Are you?"

"Sure."

"All righty, my friend. I'm going to have you count backwards for me from one hundred. Then we're going to get to work and get you back home to rest up. Sound good?"

"Yep."

"Don't worry," he assures me with a wink, "I have steady hands."

A nurse places a mask over my mouth and nose and I begin counting out loud from one hundred. I make it to ninety-six before I'm unconscious. Some time later, groggy and barely lucid, I hear a woman ask which I prefer, Sprite or Coke. I manage to mumble Sprite before I pass out again. Then I hear my mother's concerned

What Color Is Your Hoodie?

voice ask, "Buddy, are you okay?" I lose consciousness and when I wake up I'm at home in bed. It is night, and I can smell the pork chops Granny cooked for dinner. I throw back the covers, take off my gold paisley boxers and see my penis, swollen to the size of a red hot sausage, the glans wrapped in an inch of white bandages, except the layers closest to the skin, which are saturated with blood.

* * *

The practice of circumcision is centuries old. Ancient societies utilized it as both a religious rite and a rite of passage, and today it remains a meaningful religious and cultural practice all over the world. The Jewish tradition of *brit milah* dictates that newborn males be circumcised when they are eight days old in accordance with Leviticus 12:3 of the Hebrew Bible. My friend and colleague Richard Westphal has a hilarious story about attending the *bris* of his friend's grandson years ago. The entire family gathered in his friend's daughter's living room to witness the occasion and when the mohel was about to apply the perforating clamp to the baby's penis a female relative shrieked "This is torture!" and ran out of the room sobbing. This outraged sentiment is felt by an increasing number of individuals. Circumcision has been under attack in the United States for many years now, with both men and women adamantly opposed to the practice, even as part of a religious tradition. Others defend it on the grounds of personal hygiene and preventative health care and are backed by several medical studies that suggest men with a circumcised penis are less likely to contract and spread HIV and other sexually transmitted diseases. These studies also contend that circumcision significantly reduces a man's risk of penile and prostate cancer. Though not nearly as explosive as debates surrounding female circumcision, male circumcision unleashes charged emotions in virtually every person and makes each of us question topics we probably don't spend much time thinking about, chiefly sexual pleasure, reproduction, male attractiveness and sexuality, masculinity, religion, and culture. If it is true that the penis, in a metaphorical sense, is language, the fountain of paternalism in almost every culture, human beings have a great deal to communicate in how that language is conveyed and passed on. In other words, we all have a vested stake in the penis, especially—and for obvious reasons—men. The body as community property is a long held belief in fundamentalist societies, but is more focused on women's bodies than men's bodies. Yet what a man does with his penis, whether he uses it for procreation or pleasure, profit or power, has consequences that extend beyond him and into society. The tension between individual freedom and cultural expectations rests at the core of the circumcision debate as it does every topic concerning the human body.

I dislike generalizations, but I am very confident in my belief that every man is preoccupied with his penis. Regardless of their sexual orientation, race, or age, whether they exist within Western or Eastern culture, are circumcised or uncircumcised, men are enamored of their phallus and that of other men. This strong interest in the penis has a biological purpose and directly impacts human reproduction. The human penis is designed to shovel another man's semen out of his mate's womb, thereby ensuring she will bear his offspring and no other man's. Sperm competition, the desire to achieve alpha-male status and impart his genetics into future generations, drives men to want to procreate with as many women as possible. The erotic manifestation of sperm competition keeps the adult entertainment industry thriving and helps explain why so many men are aroused by pornography exhibiting gangbangs, orgies and cuckold scenarios. Given this information, circumcision makes sense, because the removal of the foreskin helps ensure that a man can father children and shovel out another man's semen. Yet the price of this reproductive advantage is decreased sensitivity during sexual intercourse and, for men who were circumcised as infants, no voice in a decision that impacts so many parts of their lives.

* * *

Unlike the women in my family, the men (what few there are) remained stone silent on the topic of my circumcision. Men typically

What Color Is Your Hoodie?

do not discuss their medical troubles, certainly not those related specifically to a men's health concern, and our silence is killing us. While women have turned breast cancer, HPV, contraception, and a host of other women's health issues into a worldwide movement, men's reluctance to openly dialogue about testicular cancer, prostate cancer, and other men's health issues only exacerbates and accelerates these illnesses. Yet in regard to circumcision this has begun to change. San Francisco recently became the nexus of a large debate concerning circumcision with groups on both sides passionately arguing their position. The San Francisco Male Genital Mutilation Bill was set to appear on an election ballot in 2011 but was struck down by Superior Court Judge Loretta Giorgi. Those who advocate for circumcision hold the opinion that the procedure has health benefits and continues religious, cultural, and family traditions. Yet those opposed to circumcision, who see it at best as invasive cosmetic surgery and at worst torture, raise valid concerns: What happens to a nation of men who have been subjected to violence hours after their birth? Could they carry the memory of it from the dawn of life into adulthood? Could all circumcised men to one degree or another be suffering from post-traumatic stress disorder? What if the puffery of hawkish presidents and bombastic business tycoons, the arrogant bravado of the wiseass in the Hummer SUV who double parks on busy streets, the alcoholic dad who slaps his kids around, or the crazed gunman who massacres scores of innocent people are actions of men reacting to the pain inflicted upon them at birth? If a boy's introduction to the world is violent, if pain is a boy's first lesson, when he masters this lesson it can result in horrific consequences for the entire population. Weighing benefits and risks, sifting through medical fact and psychological research, superstition and intuition, as a nation the United States must posit not only the necessity of circumcision but our reasons for preferring circumcised penises over ones that are not.

If we are honest with ourselves, Americans by and large will confess that a circumcised penis is more aesthetically pleasing to them than an uncircumcised one. Some would argue that a cut cock is distinctly American given that roughly fifty-seven percent of newborn males in the United States undergo circumcision. American dicks are made of tough stuff. They've spent over two centuries bouncing on horseback over rough terrain, shrinking in blizzards, sweltering in heatwaves, fighting a revolution, a civil war, wars in foreign lands, and enduring the usual biological functions. They rub against layers of clothing, both coarse and nonfibrous, all the time, losing the suppleness and sensitivity foreskin provides. Privately, I'm sure many American men would argue that cut cocks appear rugged and aggressive, not like the overly sensitive uncut cocks of European men. A European cock may be as sensitive and seductive as the man who swings it between his thighs but a cut American cock doesn't play games; it is frank, exposed and available, not sheathed in mystery or enrobed in coy flirtation. An American man will pound his sex partner like a jackhammer busting concrete because, damn it, he's got to *feel* it. The idea of American exceptionalism also extends below the belt.

In actuality, circumcision is practiced in African countries more than anywhere else, and there are particularly high occurrences in Middle Eastern nations where Islamic religious practices make circumcision compulsory. By contrast, European nations report the lowest circumcision rates worldwide. In fact, circumcision in the West is declining even in the United States, but Americans still report the highest number of circumcisions among all Western nations. Since most women and gay men in other parts of the world are comfortable engaging in sexual intercourse with uncircumcised men, if their cultural ethos touts a different ideal of male beauty and sexual desirability, why are so many American women and gay men revolted by an uncircumcised penis?

Pop culture only exacerbates anxiety over the penis. Tune in to any random sitcom and you are likely to hear at least one dick joke. Crude, sophomoric exchanges over size, color and function has profited studios, stars, and comedians millions of dollars over the years, yet dick jokes are symptomatic of the culture's widespread juvenilization. Fascination with genitals harkens back to childhood, an individual's discovery that boys are not like girls and, of course, boys are not like boys. Still, this doesn't account for the alarm

What Color Is Your Hoodie?

some Americans exhibit over an uncircumcised penis. In a notable episode of *Sex and the City*, a show which, for better or worse, branded itself as the voice of American women at the beginning of the twenty-first century, Charlotte, the most mannered and conservative-minded member of the quartet, after glimpsing her boyfriend's uncircumcised penis for the first time, gossips to her gal pals over brunch that it looked like a shar pei, her reaction as horrified as a Girl Scout who just had a clump of dog shit flung at her. A few years earlier on an episode of the low brow sitcom *Married . . . with Children,* Al Bundy was mistakenly given a circumcision after he was admitted to the hospital for back surgery (somehow the surgeon's note on Al's chart for a "circular incision" was misread as "circumcision"). For the rest of the episode Al is made the butt of one crass joke after another as his family and neighbors mock his loss of size, sensitivity, and manliness. America's hostility toward uncircumcised penises and ostricization of the men who possess them has strong roots in the nation's troubled, storied past. Just like cultural tensions surrounding race, gender, and religion, these assumptions and biases have complex origins that have proven difficult to eradicate.

Circumcision in the United States became common practice in the nineteenth century when a cultural campaign prescribing cleanliness and hygiene, both personal and moral, united the medical community and Christian moralists against any and all personal and sexual practices they viewed as unclean, thereby unhealthy and unholy. Likewise, psychologists and moral crusaders merged pseudoscience with urban myths (masturbation will cause blindness, for example) to terrorize parents into believing that circumcision would prevent sexual deviance and noisome activities in adolescent boys and young men. These ludicrous ideas persisted into the twentieth century even after sex crusaders like Alfred Kinsey dispelled them as hogwash. What Kinsey and other sexologists, psychologists, and physicians determined beyond all this falderal was the harsh reality that bias against uncircumcised men carries a xenophobic and racist subtext. As the nation experienced an immigration boom from Southern and Eastern Europe in the late nineteenth century, the rise in prejudice against these groups assumed many complex forms. In regard to immigrant men, many of whom came from cultures where circumcision was not practiced, native-born Americans perpetuated ugly stereotypes that these men's bodies were filthy and disease-ridden, as evidenced by their foreskin. In Europe the opposite was true: during the rise of Nazism a circumcised penis became a litmus test to determine if a man was of Jewish extraction, making him a candidate for extermination. Bodies on trial. Bodies at mercy. Bodies marked for death.

* * *

The stitches have fallen out, the swelling has subsided and the redness has vanished. I can wear briefs again, walk without wincing, shower and know that every single part of my body is clean. For the first time I can urinate in a steady stream; my fear of urinals is gone. And now, after weeks of abstinence, my penis can become my pleasure once more. Until the man I desire comes to me, my own body must substitute for him, supply both the source of my lust and its attendant satisfaction.

It is late, Granny is asleep, and the house is quite. My bedroom is aglow with light flickering from the porn on my television, the acrobatics of impossibly beautiful men with gladiatorial physiques fucking with joyous abandon. Fully erect, I reach for my penis and begin the usual manipulations. After three weeks of abstinence my body is beckoning for a much needed release but I quickly realize that the circumcision, while making my member function properly, has also made it foreign to me. I am no more in tuned to my body and its functions than I was before the surgery. My penis chafes; it is less sensitive. The men in the porn flick continue their manic fucking, a sight so arousing I'm filled with jealousy that I cannot join them, even by proxy. It takes several minutes—much longer than it ever has before—to teach myself new methods of self-pleasure: new places to apply pressure, different rhythms. Still, I cannot achieve the same pleasure. Then I remember what the pamphlet Dr. Elkins gave me weeks ago suggested, words he himself spoke to me during

WHAT COLOR IS YOUR HOODIE?

our last consultation. I rise from my bed, enter the bathroom next to my bedroom and open the cabinet beneath the sink. There among rolls of toilet paper, witch hazel, cleanser, body lotion and Lysol I find it—baby oil.

* * *

For African Americans, the topic of circumcision is just as divisive as it is for the rest of the nation. As people with a longstanding mistrust of the medical community, this is not surprising. From the ignominy of the Tuskegee syphilis experiment to their delayed response to the HIV/AIDS crisis in the African American community, blacks have been loath to place too much faith in doctors. Circumcising their infant sons was not a priority for many black parents, and those who had no qualms about the procedure may not have been able to afford it, certainly not my teenage mother or her parents, who had to survive on Granddaddy's pay as a non-union trash collector. Interestingly, most of the black men I've seen who are not circumcised tend to be older and primarily from the South. According to the Center for Disease Control and Prevention, from the late 1970s to the late 1990s black infants were seven percent less likely to be circumcised than whites. But today both races are on par in terms of the rate of circumcision, and those rates are declining. Still, I question the cultural mix contributing to stigmatization in this regard, and I don't think it's too much of a stretch to believe that limiting or denying access to circumcision by both blacks and whites amplifies exoticization of black men.

* * *

This is the story I pieced together from snatches of recollections offered by various family members; this is the story that seems most plausible to me. My mother concealed her pregnancy from my father, her family and friends for the first six months of her pregnancy. Brian, my father, who was captain of the football team at the same high school where my mother was a varsity cheerleader, told me once that he would take her on dates in early autumn and she'd wear her heavy winter coat. Perplexed by this, when he questioned her about it her snippy reply would always be, "I'm cold. Can't I be cold?"

When her parents discovered my mother was pregnant, my grandfather beat her with a thick leather belt until one of her brother's restrained him. Mama is the seventh of eight children, and Granddaddy, a man with a sixth grade education, owing to dirt poor country superstition and a drunk's whiskey-soaked logic, called her his lucky child, the one he knew would accomplish great things.

I was born prematurely on a Friday afternoon, the first day in March. When Mama brought me home from the hospital my grandfather, pleased to finally have a grandson after four granddaughters, looked me over and, surprised at my small size, said, "He's a little peewee." After thirty-nine years, this is the name all of my family members still call me. They seem to glory in the nickname, swirling it in their mouths like fine wine. Growing up, I was terrified of an aunt or cousin accidentally slipping and calling me Peewee in front of friends. Peewee was my bad name, the persona I inhabited only in the strict company of my family, the only people in the world who knew that as a boy I regularly pretended to be Barbara Eden in *I Dream of Jeannie* and that the first summer I had roller skates I skated in the grass on my grandparents' front lawn for fear of falling on the sidewalk. It never occurred to anyone during my childhood or pubescence that calling a boy Peewee during his formative years could have a detrimental psychological impact. They meant no harm, yet by the time this was brought to light it was too late for all of us. Though some relatives have grudgingly set aside Peewee for Jarrett, others simply refuse to give up Peewee, as if doing so will erase the memory of my childhood from their minds. For them Peewee has become my name, and like disgraced Congressman Anthony Weiner my name is bound to phallic imagery and fodder for mockery and shame. Yet Peewee is more than that.

Peewee is a boy who spends too much time alone.

Peewee is a welfare lullaby for teen mothers living in the ghetto.

What Color Is Your Hoodie?

Peewee is the sound of a father giving up and a grandfather not even trying.

Peewee is a body under threat.

As hard as I try cannot recall what prompted me to seek out a physician all those years ago and get a circumcision. For twenty years I had managed to adjust to the limits phimosis had placed on how I urinated, masturbated, and conducted myself as a male, never considering how it would impact my life once I began having sex. Yet some men with phimosis manage to conduct vital sex lives without ever going under the knife. Even my journals from that time in my life offer nothing in the way of a definitive moment that prompted my stealthy visit to Dr. O'Connor. Yet if a reason can be deduced, I think, after a failed year at college that coincided with the realization of my homosexuality, having the surgery was my first step toward self-acceptance and reclamation, a way of wresting control of my identity, body, sexuality and destiny from my family, my community, and the culture. The black penis is a site of multiple political, cultural and historical battles. Masculinity in general begins and ends with the penis, yet men of African descent are constrained by the stereotypes assigned to our bodies by racist hegemonic forces prevalent throughout Western culture. The psychological tug of war we experience, our bleak history of exploitation, mutilation, shaming, and murder, links directly to white hegemonic lust and hysteria over our genitals, yielding from the legacy of slavery and Jim Crow. From the garrulous halls of academia to the orgasmic moans that score pornographic films splashed across the Internet, black men and our genitals have absorbed so much debate and dialogue, fetishization and envy that it's a wonder any of us keep our sanity. To be left alone with one's body and to be in sole possession of it, disconnected from the stereotypes, assumptions and expectations tethering it to society, is a glorious feeling. Yet, sadly, most black men never truly experience it. Individuals who stand in opposition to infant circumcision comprehend this desire, and their stance in this regard should not be challenged.

And yet my private feelings about circumcision as a medical procedure apart from aesthetics and cultural or religious practices conflict with these ideas. The circumcision debate presents worthy arguments on all sides. For private reasons I have decided to live child-free, yet if I had a newborn son, loving him as much as my mother loves me and full of the first-hand knowledge I have about the procedure and the physical and psychological effects it has on a male, knowledge my teenage mother lacked at the time of my birth, I would elect to have my son circumcised. My circumstances were rare; most men aren't given the opportunity to live part of their adult lives both cut and uncut, and I feel incredibly lucky that I have. I had a choice about my surgery, and I made the right choice. But what is more important than the circumcision itself, more important than how I perceive my body now, is the pride I can take in owning it and the decisions I make regarding what I will and will not do with it. Perhaps it has always been about my body, this restlessness within me that I have scrawled onto countless reams of paper, expressed in essays, journals, stories, and poems. Perhaps now, finally, the needs of my body, the urgency of my convictions and the expression of my desires will align, each serving the other and all serving a good that extends beyond me.

What Color Is Your Hoodie?

Little black boys seldom smile. The boys on the West side of Chicago bundled in coats as puffy as their cocoa cheeks who sit on the Green Line with their mamas and big sisters; the ones ambling through the breakfast cereal aisle at Price Chopper in Kansas City; the ones pacing empty rainswept playgrounds waiting, still waiting, for a relative to pick them up after school—none of them smile.

My cousin Chanda's youngest son Drew recently completed his first semester at a small college in St. Joseph, Missouri. His parents both dropped out of college when his mother became pregnant with his older brother AJ just one year shy of completing her degree. With a history of poverty, domestic instability, and a lethal package of social plagues and pressures strapped to his back, the fact that Drew successfully gained admittance to a four-year university is a monumental accomplishment. At Christmas dinner I asked him about his first semester. He told me he wanted to transfer to the University of Missouri Kansas City and live with his mother, claiming that he was more likely to find a job in Kansas City, either part-time or full-time. Like a character in an indie film, a swift montage of images flickered in my mind: Drew transferring schools, oversleeping and missing a class, then another, then another before dropping out altogether, moving in with a girl, getting her pregnant, breaking up with her and moving out, sleeping on his mother's couch, spending his days watching crap television, roaming the streets, looking for and finding trouble. He wants to major in psychology. He wants to be a counselor.

Six weeks before Drew began college, George Zimmerman

was found not guilty of murdering Trayvon Martin, a boy exactly Drew's age who died simply because he was black. The facts of the case are well-known and have been widely reported. Trayvon walks home in the rain in a Florida community that has experienced a rash of burglaries. Zimmerman, spying on Trayvon through a window in his home, calls the police to report a suspicious looking black man wearing a hoodie roaming the neighborhood. Against the 9-1-1 dispatcher's orders and all common sense, Zimmerman, armed with a nine millimeter semi-automatic pistol, the Kel-Tec PF-9, stalks Trayvon through the neighborhood. A confrontation occurs, a struggle ensues, one of them cries for help, the gun fires, and young Trayvon lies lifeless on the pavement. The succession of legal, political, and social events which transpired in the months following this horrific event enacted an all too familiar narrative: impassioned rallies and protests, public mourning, accusations of racism vaunted from every region of the culture, and endless debates regarding gun rights, youth culture, racism, black manhood, and the pervasiveness of violence throughout the United States, yet all of it is meaningless.

Trayvon Martin is dead, George Zimmerman is a free man, and I am angry.

If Americans in the twenty-first century have learned anything from this tragic circumstance it is that we've learned absolutely nothing from history. History repeats itself as predictably as the seasons change, yet we are none the wiser for our collective acknowledgment of this fact. White men kill black men regularly and, as Trayvon Martin's murder trial makes clear, they have legal authorization to do so. As so many Americans of all races and backgrounds have opined, Stand Your Ground is twenty-first century lynching hooded in huffy conservative social policy. Call it radical individualism or an extreme expression of one's constitutional rights, but when armed white men are accorded the freedom to gun down any individual who makes them feel threatened or afraid all citizens are at risk. Conservatives, libertarians, and gun rights activists who extol the belief that broadening gun rights will equalize our society and result in safer communities either do not know or refuse to acknowledge that such measures protect and embolden racist hegemonic forces and places racial and sexual minorities at grave risk. Violence has always been the most expedient method of exterminating threats to patriarchal control, and for anyone to infer that our justice system would have exonerated Trayvon Martin had the situation been reversed that tragic February night reflects an unpardonable blindness to the insidiousness of racism within Western society. The Zimmerman verdict was also a verdict for all black men, a decisive, damning verdict. The jury's acquittal merely confirmed truths black men already knew: we represent the greatest threat to white patriarchal control, and to the dominant culture our lives are cheap. Any method white society employs to eradicate us, to them, is justified.

    This fact doesn't even begin to address the black on black violence that has turned the streets of Chicago and so many other cities into war zones. After centuries of absorbing an amalgam of vile racist messages, many young black men, who lack education, positive role models, and nurturing support networks, not only believe their own lives are worthless but that all human life is worthless. Self-worth, empathy, and compunction have been subtracted from their consciousness, and their powerlessness manifests in gun violence, drug and alcohol abuse, HIV/AIDS, incarceration, and suicide. Intraracial violence confirms a host of stereotypes attributed to black men and our supposed animalism and handily takes the responsibility of exterminating black people away from white society. Reinforced by the echo chamber of hip hop which promulgates the philosophy of "keeping it real," African American men in the twenty-first century increasingly find themselves their own worst enemy, unlike earlier generations of black men who relied on one another to migrate from the Jim Crow South, educate themselves, secure gainful employment, and maintain close familial bonds. When black men neglect our children, turn our backs on our community, exhibit and defend stereotypical behavior, perpetuate sexism and homophobia, turn our backs on education, and fail to love ourselves we give credence to centuries of abuses. When black men resolve to get rich or die trying we've already killed ourselves, and white supremacist patriarchy wins. The tragedy of Trayvon Martin is the unending tragedy of America. To black men across the country, Trayvon's murder reminds us in chilling, nightmarish fashion that we are not safe, that we have never been safe. Despite our social, political, and economic triumphs over the last half century, nothing can protect black men from the violence of racism.

Hatred is hatred no matter what form it takes. The murderous impulses that ended Trayvon Martin's life are the same ones that took the life of Matthew Shepard, Brandon Tina, and so many other LGBT individuals. Annihilation of the other by any means necessary is, was, and always will be the primary goal of white supremacist patriarchy. Sanctioned abuses to civil rights and human rights, an inability to empathize with others and fear of their own humanity exposes the dominant culture's weakness yet sets the course for its calculated assault on racial, sexual, and economic "others," a grand design that succeeds when they segregate our culture from theirs, create divisions within our own culture, divide each of us from our individual quest for happiness, and construct institutional barriers to equality. For the subaltern, the United States is not a land of asylum and opportunity. It is a wilderness rife with danger and death.

I hear all kinds of stories. An old acquaintance named Taylor admitted that he had to change clothes before he returned to his neighborhood on the South side, shed his argyle cardigan and skinny jeans in the men's locker room at our high end Near North gym and wade into baggy Dickies, a fat man's plain white T, and a black hoodie. During a job interview Wallace's potential boss freely admitted to being a racist. "I hate niggers," he said as breezily as if he was ordering seafood salad, "but I can tell you're different." This incident took place twenty-four hours before George Zimmerman was acquitted of murdering Trayvon Martin seventy yards from his back door.

The night before he began his first day of college I wrote Drew a letter listing ten strategies he needed to follow in order to be a

What Color Is Your Hoodie?

successful student, among them setting aside time to read each day and visiting his professors regularly during office hours. The tenth and last dictum was to use a condom, a directive I wrote five times with the broad side of a black Sharpie in boxy uppercase letters. I am proudly sex positive and champion sexual freedom and expression for all people each chance I get. I know sex can have dire consequences. After spending a lifetime hearing one sad story after another involving a promising young person whose chances to succeed were squashed because of sexual ignorance or irresponsibility, I feel it is the duty of the African American and LGBT communities to continue our efforts to educate our youth about the pitfalls of such behavior. We have to teach both young black men and gay men not to buy into the myth of hypersexuality ascribed to both groups and to value their bodies and the bodies of their partners. We have to encourage them to view unprotected sex as a benefit of monogamy, social responsibility, and good health. We have to make them despise unplanned pregnancy, STIs, and HIV/AIDS. If we want them to use protection we have to make them understand that their lives are worth protecting.

The urgency of communicating this message to young black gay men, who continue to contract HIV at an alarming rate, cannot be underestimated. We in the gay community need look no further than pornography to understand how dire this situation is. The number of black men performing in bareback porn is alarming. Although pornography can no more model healthy sexual relationships than television sitcoms can pattern stable, loving relationships, the growing number of black men performing in bareback porn suggests to viewers that the lives of black gay men are not worth protecting, that we are complicit in our own demise and have become our own worst enemy, making it nearly impossible for gay African American men to trust one another. Ironically, one of the main reasons HIV rates remain so high among African American men is that most black gay and bisexual men (and those on the down low) engage in sex with other black men. Our sex, rather than being the loving revolution Marlon Riggs claimed it should be, is killing us.

Homophobia undoubtedly contributes greatly to the escalation of HIV/AIDS transmissions within our population yet this is only part of the problem. Cross-cultural redefinitions of manhood are necessary in combating the virus as well as the ignorance and shame attached to it. So long as black men find themselves struggling to obtain an education and secure employment that will compensate them livable wages and adequate health care, they will be vulnerable to contracting the virus. The concept of manhood, in the wake of the Great Recession, the current wave of feminism, and the advancement of gay rights and multiculturalism, has men of every race, age, class, orientation, and religious affiliation scrambling to determine just what makes a man a man in the twenty-first century and, sadly, promiscuity and sexual irresponsibility assumes the form of masculine identity for a number of men regardless of sexual orientation. They have no other way to prove their manhood and know of no path toward healthy expressions of manhood. Despite cultural dialogue about multiculturalism and manhood over the last forty years, black gangbangers still gun down other black gangbangers wearing the wrong colored hoodie in the wrong hood. Latino men express so much terror of being feminized they refuse to ride the Pink Line L-train in Chicago, and trigger happy white men stalk suburban streets, eager to assassinate anyone with black or brown skin.

Some of my students gasped when they saw the photos in the power point presentation—black men who had been tortured and mutilated, their necks secured in nooses, their bullet-ridden bodies dangling from the boughs of trees, their genitals cut off and stuffed in their mouths. Throngs of white people stand below pointing and smiling as wide as Christmas morning.

I was vacationing in Brazil with my husband when I heard the news about Paula Deen. The Internet was agog with the scandal of the Southern chef's blithe admission in a legal deposition to referring to black people as niggers. She even expressed her desire for an antebellum Southern-themed wedding complete with black people acting as slaves. Weepy and guilt-ridden, she made the

What Color Is Your Hoodie?

rounds on daytime talk shows to apologize to the public and beg forgiveness, yet in true American fashion her mea culpa contained a nugget of egotistical defiance when some time later she asserted, "I is what I is." Paula Deen's admissions surprised relatively few African Americans. Coming just one month before George Zimmerman's acquittal and two months before the fiftieth anniversary of the March on Washington, racism had become the nation's hot topic that season and just about everyone was about to swallow a scalding cupful of it.

In a summer where I lamented the Supreme Court's decision to gut the Voting Rights Act of 1965 but applauded their decision to overturn the Defense of Marriage Act and Prop. 8, once again I found myself torn between allegiances: dejected as a black man, euphoric as a gay man, and troubled as an American. Suffrage and marriage gird citizenship; they offer protection from an accumulation of society's ills, allow free expression of individual desire, and equalize citizens in a society that is becoming increasingly, frighteningly, unequal. The decades long struggle for African Americans to freely exercise their voting rights and have their marriages recognized by every governing body within the nation demonstrates the black race's will to power and our determination never to afford our oppressors the satisfaction of seeing us resigned to defeat. Those of us who inhabit the intersection of black and gay identities, because of the Supreme Court's ruling, have been placed in uncomfortable circumstances yet again, our hearts and bodies yet again disconnected as we vacillate between shouts of joy and wails of sorrow, unsure whether to dance on tabletops or march in the streets. More and more it is becoming clear to me and others that to be a black gay man in the United States is to be stalked, targeted, and placed under suspicion. It also means learning to keep one's innermost feelings in check, to find an unhappy equilibrium between joy and sorrow, loneliness and community, acceptance and rejection. Once he comes to an awareness of his sexual orientation, a black gay man quickly learns to fragment himself, to place his own feelings aside so that other people can be comfortable. Suspect everyone. Trust no one.

Yet this is no way to live. How can I wish damnation upon

every Caucasian I see when the person I love most in this world is a white man? How can I defend black men against charges of barbarity when I know that given the right circumstances many of them would call me a faggot and assault me and my husband? How can I attend a five hundred dollar a plate HRC fundraiser when I know most of the gay white men around me would assume I paid for my dinner with my cock?

As a small boy I wasn't allowed in my grandparents' bedroom. I assumed it was because they didn't want me looking at the layer of glossy porn magazines Granddaddy kept beneath the mattress. I never even considered the bottle of Hennessey or the loaded .357.

I was summoned to the dean's office after I copied him a rather brusque email I sent to a professor. The facts of the exchange are not so very important; the professor made a request, and in a charged tone I now concede lacked my usual diplomacy and professionalism, I declined. What the dean assumed would be a quick ten minute meeting admonishing me for my lapse in diplomacy resulted in a two hour showdown during which we each unleashed years of personal and profession slights, accusations, and aspersions. The most damning charge he made against me was that he expressed his fear of being alone in his office with me, implying that I might fly into a violent rage. It was the first time in my life I had ever had that accusation hurled at me, and it stung. The fact that someone I had known and worked with for seven years, a man I had come to think of as a mentor and friend, someone highly educated who should have known better, could think of me as a monstrous black brute who would unleash violence upon him sent me reeling. I couldn't eat for days after this meeting, and my stress and anxiety amplified when my own husband sided with him, claiming that indeed I have moments when my anger seethes and finds chilling expression in my face and comportment. The more I thought about it the more I realized this is the standard white response whenever African Americans assert ourselves, express dissatisfaction, or rebel against the oppressive forces of white supremacy. Dismissing African Americans as pathologically

What Color Is Your Hoodie?

angry and threatening is easier for white people than acknowledging, correcting, and apologizing for discrimination and injustice. *Angry* and *threatening* are pejorative terms meant to destabilize black progress. These words reflect patriarchy's demonstration of power over subalterns. Think of it: When black men get angry we are incarcerated, expelled from society, or killed. When white men get angry, however, people die. White men are the ones who storm into movie theatres, schools, and other public spaces, open fire and slaughter scores of innocent people. White men were the ones who traveled to foreign lands and brought with them violence, slavery, disease, rape, and torture. A white man's anger is allowed to manifest in innumerable ways and assume countless forms, but the anger of black men and all men of color must be contained and if it cannot be contained it must be quashed. Likewise, the man who expresses such anger must also be destroyed lest any of his brethren feel emboldened to lash out as well. *Angry* and *threatening* are verbal nooses, hoodies of a lingual variety.

But if I am angry, so what? Does being a black man mean I am not entitled to anger the way others are? Anger is an unhealthy emotion but necessary, I think, in some circumstances. If nothing else anger serves as an instinctual reaction to injustice, for any action which elevates the status of one person while simultaneously lowering that of another, any action which satisfies one person through impugning another, any demonstration that gratifies one in order to deprive the other is an injustice.

The foundation of diasporic black male psychology is rooted in slavery, genocide, and disenfranchisement. Given our traumatic introduction to this culture it should come as no surprise that paranoia is a common experience for black men. We fear and we are afraid. Black men spend much of our lives managing rage and fear, fighting the impulse to harm or self-harm. Cornell West writes, "[t]he accumulated effect of the black wounds and scars suffered in a white-dominated society is a deep-seated anger, a boiling sense of rage, and a passionate pessimism regarding America's will to justice."[15] Most black men I know, at one time or another, have

---

15. Cornell West. 2001. *Race Matters*. Beacon Press: Boston. 18.

been in therapy; I am no exception. Yet we are lucky. We possess access to mental health services and the presence of mind to seek out individuals who can help us cope with life in a society that wishes nothing but the worst for us. But most African American men either don't have access to these services or resist consulting a psychotherapist due to cultural barriers and masculine pride. Black men across the diaspora find ourselves constrained by feelings of fear and self-hatred. Canadian writer Orville Lloyd Douglas, in a short yet controversial article title "Why I Hate Being a Black Man," succulently addresses this issue: "A lot of the time I feel like my skin color is like my personal prison, something that I have no control over, for I am judged just for the way I look. No[,] discussing the issue doesn't mean it is going to go away. In fact, by ignoring the issue it simply lurks underneath the surface. I believe a dialogue about self-hatred should be brought to the fore in the public sphere, so that some sort of healing and the development of true nonlabel-based pride can occur."[16] Black men learn self-hatred from the day we are born. No matter what we achieve or acquire we are constantly reminded that we owe all of our accomplishments, in one way or another, to a group of people who once owned our ancestors, people like my dean who think we need to be managed, and people like George Zimmerman who want to kill each and every one of us.

She approaches from the opposite direction taking measured steps in orthopedic shoes, shrunken and stooped, colorless wrinkled skin, snow white hair cut in a pageboy. Not a new situation for me. I know the drill: eyes forward, don't walk too slow or too fast, keep my hands visible and at my sides. I'm so proud to be wearing my Barack Obama T-shirt just days after the inauguration I want to tear it from my torso and wave it like a flag. She looks at the shirt then up at me. "Another one," she growls as she passes.

---

16. Orville Lloyd Douglas. November 13, 2013. "Why I Hate Being a Black Man". The Root. http://www.theroot.com/articles/culture/2013/11/_why_i_hate_being_a_black_man.2.html.

What Color Is Your Hoodie?

I sit on my couch in the middle of the night in the middle of a freezing December, the close of an auspicious year that began with Barack Obama's second inauguration and ended with Nelson Mandela's death. A copy of Kiese Laymon's *How to Slowly Kill Yourself and Others in America* lays beside me, and I wonder how many more essays like this have to be written before men like me will be safe in this nation. Methods and modes of resistance to white racist patriarchal forces transfigure over time. From migration to protests, authorship to violence, the black community has many means to combat its enemies, yet despite the battles we have won the war against oppression goes on. Some things are certain: when black men forge and maintain inclusive communities we strengthen our bonds. When black men of all classes, orientations and expressions of gender enter healthy loving relationships our enemies are weakened. I realize that my writing, Laymon's collection of essays, and the writing of other black men—Hilton Als, Keith Boykin, Ellis Cose, Dwight McBride, Robert Reid-Phar, Touré, Thomas Chatterton Williams—proves that the white supremacist culture we live in does not have to power to claim us all. When black men write we fortify ourselves and our community against the world's racism. When black men write we strengthen our fraternal bonds and white racist patriarchy grows fearful. Black men must write.

These same prescriptions apply to gay men. Sharing our stories, memorializing our victories and injustices, communicating the details of our lives to straight society and rebelling against homophobia and heterosexism, even in small ways, helps to galvanize our community and fortify us against the world's prejudices. Yet we must first speak out against injustices within the LGBT community to achieve these aims. When our community overcomes class and racial tensions and truly embraces diversity we can combat homophobia. Many in the LGBT community feel our focused attention on marriage equality is misplaced and that other issues, such as an end to workplace discrimination and more attention to combating HIV/AIDS, should be the first priority of the Gay Rights movement. This argument is sound. Yet as critical as these other issues are to advancing the movement, being able to refer to my husband as my husband imparts great power to me and Gerald, and the power of language should never be dismissed. "Husband" tripping from a gay man's lips has multiple employments—it is a weapon and a shield, wealth and currency, testament and prophecy. Each time I utter "husband" I fire a bullet into patriarchy.

They shanté up to Boystown on hot sticky July nights because they'll get their asses kicked or worse in Austin or Englewood. One long ride on the Red Line transforms them from faggots to fabulous, from bitch ass niggas to catch of the day. Bodies once destined to lie in a crime scene are now lethal weapons, sparkling, flawless. For them Halsted Street is more than a strip of bars where bare chested pretty white boys grind and gyrate on platforms while silver-haired daddies sip overpriced cocktails and leer. It is a runway, a safe passage, a birth canal. Ladyboys strut in Nine West heels and mopped Deréon jeans, swing their yaki ombre weave and padded hips. His stomach may have forgotten what solid food is but her body is sickening. Somebody's grandson is now somebody's grand diva throwing more shade than Beyoncé at the bouncer for his obvious ignorance. Rumors of black men charged twice the normal cover to enter a gay bar. Queens deposed. Truths exposed. Don't try it, little boy. You'll get read to filth.

Protection comes in many forms: mace, knives, guns, muscles, solidarity. It is no accident that gay men cluster in the same areas throughout the nation. Unlike African Americans who, before the Fair Housing Act of 1968, had no choice but to remain segregated from the rest of society, gays transcend every socioeconomic class and come from every region. Fleeing violently homophobic gun happy small towns and rural communities, we conglomerate in gay neighborhoods like Boystown, Dupont Circle, and Castro for protection as much as kinship, yet safety is an illusion, a state of mind. Halsted Street on a raucous Saturday night in July can be just as dangerous to a gay man as the prairies surrounding Laramie,

What Color Is Your Hoodie?

Wyoming and the rain-slick sidewalks of Sanford, Florida. Our enemies know where to find us. But even within our community threats exist.

Classism, racism, and stigmatization of those living with HIV/AIDS thrive within the gay community with men of color routinely on the receiving end of these injustices. Just as black men are often forced to alter themselves in myriad ways to fit into the dominate culture and protect themselves against white supremacy, black gay men must often manage the dual challenge of transforming themselves to fit into mainstream gay society which is dominated by upper income white men and cordoned off to the rest of the gay community. Black gay men have mastered the art of shape-shifting, altering our bodies, speech, mannerisms, and wardrobe in order to maintain kinship with the African American community and be recognized by groups like the Human Rights Campaign which claim to speak for the entire LGBT community. Yet LGBT people of color often express frustration at feeling overlooked by this group and the men and women who belong to it. Many black gay men simply refuse to play the game and actively oppose the gay mainstream, forging their own subculture within the subculture. Other black gay men, rebelling against stigmatization and homophobia within the black community, embrace the gay mainstream and the process of "cloning" they must undergo. In this respect the gay community is no different than any other group. Like Trayvon Martin's hoodie, the article of clothing that falsely marked him as a thug, a threat, and a miscreant by George Zimmerman and every other racist monster in America, our identity is as much our own original creation as it is an amalgam of assumptions and stereotypes we either conform to, react against, or reappropriate. At various times in our lives we all cloak ourselves in the same metaphorical hoodie whether the forces of our inequitable society impose it upon us or we conceal ourselves in it of our own free will, an act of rebellion or survival.

We were sleeping with the same white guy who had a long term partner living in another city. I was new to the rotation, twenty-two, and fresh out of the closet. When he couldn't reach me he'd called

Jamari. When Jamari threw hissy fits, our mutual fuck buddy would invite me to his house for a homemade Italian dinner and Chianti. We wound up in bed every time. Once, I arrived too early. Jamari, fuming, was on his way out; I was strolling in. I said hello to him as he plodded through the doorway and a thousand deaths shot from his eyes. Later, in bed, the man we were sharing said, "Never mind him. He hates you just because you're younger, taller, and light-skinned."

Regardless of our politics, region, class or sexual orientation, African American men find common ground and common strength in alterity. Even the most rabid homophobe or strident conservative among us recognizes that black men, as a group, continue to endure discrimination within a system which seeks to destroy us. That we survive at all is a miracle given the host of economic, social, and political machinations working against us. Unity is the strongest weapon against an oppressive system; this has been proven again and again throughout history. That destabilizing influences such as homophobia, classism, and lack of education continue to thrive within the black community signifies the work we must continue to do to ensure every one of us, our lives and histories, is validated, respected, and protected. All means all.

Year after year I see young black men like Drew crash and burn in college. I was one of them. Confusion over my sexual orientation contributed to my initial failure in college, yet ironically, embracing my homosexuality and finding a loving partner motivated me to return to college and successfully complete my studies. Education and solidarity are the only remedy for the ills that plague black men and gay men, the only path out of the destructive cycles that keep most of us unemployed, addicted, or incarcerated. When black men and gay men love themselves unconditionally and embrace the totality of our experiences we fortify ourselves against multiple evils.

Most folks wear them for style and comfort, not protection from inclement weather. Mine is slate gray. It shrunk in the wash a long time ago but if I wear it often enough, flex my elbows and tug at

What Color Is Your Hoodie?

the sleeves repeatedly, it will eventually regain its usual fit. On a cold rainy night it feels good to zip myself in it while I slouch on the sofa, watch black and white movies, and eat hot soup. Young guys at the gym wear them quite often, even in summer when it seems the last thing anyone would want to do is layer. And let's not forgot the world of hip hop which started the trend: brothas skilled in verbal gymnastics, their flesh tattooed with more ink than a dissertation, hardcore and fabulously hood transforming the hood of a sweatshirt from utility to crown. The halo of an avenging angel. The cowl of a cunning bandit. The cape of a superhero. The mythic cloak of invisibility. Hood up/hood down—they see him only when he wants them to. Rogue or Romeo, they can't catch his swagger. They never could.

Bibliography

Douglas, Orville Lloyd. November 13, 2013. "Why I Hate Being a Black Man". The Root. http://www.theroot.com/articles/culture/2013/11/_why_i_hate_being_a_black_man.2.html.

West, Cornell. 2001. *Race Matters*. Beacon Press: Boston.

OUR FIERCE COMMUNITY

"We are the ones we have been waiting for."
—Barack Obama, February 18, 2008

"There's no such thing as a colored fag."

Carroll O'Connor, playing Archie Bunker, one of television's most iconic characters, delivered this line of dialogue during the fifth season of the critically acclaimed sitcom *All in the Family*, which broke new ground for its incisive critique of American culture during the 1970s, a turbulent decade in which the nation grappled with the Watergate Scandal, the Vietnam War, the social rebellion of women, blacks, and gays, and the sexual revolution, all unfolding amid economic inflation, a gas crisis, and mounting crime in cities across the country. The genius of the show and the reason it remains a trenchant critique of American society even today is that the joke was always on Archie Bunker, the chubby blue collar conservative bigot who spouted asinine malapropisms as regularly as he voided his bowels. "There's no such thing as a colored fag" was Archie's rejoinder to his liberal son-in-law Mike's (Rob Reiner) vehement defense of homosexuals and racial diversity within the gay community, an ignorant pronouncement Archie supports by expressing, "Walk up to any colored guy and ask him, 'Are you a fag?' Your tonsils will be wearing your mustache." Though exposing Archie's ignorance is the main point of this exchange, the subtext of his remarks unmasks the larger, complex question of cultural visibility. As an enduring symbol of the dominant culture—middle-aged heterosexual white men—Archie Bunker in 1974, just as he does today, reflects their views as well as their modus operandi. Not only does he deny black gay men's existence, he concedes that even if patriarchy chooses to acknowledge us they will relegate us to second class citizens, in effect rendering us non-people. The reality that masculine, healthy, politically and socially engaged black gay men exist is unconscionable to the Archie Bunkers of the world. Moreover, Archie's assertion that a black man would violently assault anyone for questioning his sexuality speaks to white culture's need to stereotype black men as violent, reactionary, hypersexual brutes who lack impulse control and exhibit even more homophobia than whites. In a time before civil rights, affirmative action, social integration, and multiculturalism became firmly rooted in the American body politic, black gay men, like all other minority groups, found themselves ghettoized to a space so distant from the center of cultural and political discourse, so confined within the narrow periphery of white supremacist patriarchy, that Archie and his cohorts could only envision us as spooks howling from the echo chamber of urban legends.

But Archie Bunker is right. In truth there is no such thing as a colored fag. From what I have heard, from the details I have compiled over the years like scientific observations hastily scribbled on the blue-lined pages of marbled black-and-white composition books, colored fags only come out at night. Their effect on people differs: white men cackle hysterically at the sight of them while they generate ungovernable rage within black men. White women pity them and black women pray for them. A relative once told me colored fags don't know if they want to be men or women but she wished they would just go to church and pray. A classmate qualified this sentiment years later when he opined that colored fags really wanted to be women; his friend corrected him, stating that colored fags had both a penis and a vagina. Coworkers once swore to me colored fags have anal sex with gerbils, all of them, without exception. I am told they suffer from multiple illness, that a deadly virus thrives within their DNA, and they are eager to inflict it upon the populous. Apparently they are drug addicted and mentally ill. They cannot be trusted.

What Color Is Your Hoodie?

Estimating this construction on such grossly inflammatory, specious merits, colored fags can potentially comprise a vast, eclectic amalgamation of self-destructive people meting out a slim existence on the fringe of society. The colored fags conjured by the racist homophobes of the world inhabit the same la-la land where African slaves expressed nothing but contentment with their lot; where every woman's secret ambition is to rid herself of every shred of feminism, bear a dozen children, and submit to her husband's will; where gay men just haven't found the right woman, and all of us, individually or collectively, directly or indirectly, are ruining this country. Bigfoot and the Loch Ness Monster stand a better chance of being acknowledged by this culture. But we, the self-possessed men who glory in every shade of black and brown, who declare boundless love for one another, stride through each day in running shoes, oxfords, or stilettos, ready to wage war and declare victory, who plan grand entrances and elusive escapes, the men who somehow forge ahead when there really, truly, is no path to take, yes, we exist.

Our origins are unknown but we have always been here. Always. We predate nations and war, language and history, gender and sexuality. Chained in the hull of slave ships that tore a bloody path of sorrow across the Atlantic Ocean, we endured. Tortured and enslaved, sold and bred like livestock, separated from our family and even ourselves, we endured. Denied education and labor, used for our bodies and little more, we endured. Betrayed by our brothers and sisters, mocked by our religion, we endured. Ravaged by plague, we endured. Ours is the greatest love story of the world, the example for countless star-crossed lovers. Our clandestine lovers—the men we proudly took to bed, to heart, and to mind; the continent we once ruled more like gods than kings; the mighty nation we constructed acre by acre with our bare hands and populated with millions of sons and daughters—were snatched from our embrace so long ago memory weeps for what it can no longer offer us. Yet this has not deterred us. Our passage through the tumult of history has fortified us against the venality of the world and its calculated assaults. We are shielded by grace and armed with love. We have come this far by faith.

The intersection of African American and homosexual identities affords black gay men a unique vantage point from which to observe and critique culture within the United States. For us, questions of race, gender, and sexual orientation commix in a potent cocktail that we swallow each day, both enjoying and fearing the burn as it travels down into our bellies, scorching every vital organ along the way. The properties of one belong to the other. This, perhaps, is what inspires such animosity toward black gay men: we occupy the space where black people and gay people, arguably the most reviled groups in Western culture, overlap. Rather than succumbing to the ire and injustice continually lobbed at both groups, we chose to marshal it. The fear the dominant culture has of us is in fact a fear of its own maltreatments, a fear of skillfully plotted revenge. Yet what our enemies don't realize is that we have already exacted our revenge: We are alive, we are unified, and we are thriving.

Who are we? I will tell you.

We are the old men who live alone in studio apartments at the top of a dark staircase in buildings most people thought were condemned. We are the cousins and nephews only grandmothers remember to call on our birthdays. We are the men who taught you how to read, how to change a tire, how to apply your make up, how to sing in the church choir. We are the men who love women more than the men who love women. We are liberals and conservatives, populists and libertarians. We come from Thirty-ninth and Prospect in Kansas City, Eighty-fourth and Drexel in Chicago, the garrulous streets of Salvador in Brazil, dusty roads in Uganda. We ride the tube from Leicester Square to Brixton, travel to Berlin on the ICE. We'll strip down to a thong and give you a private dance at Stock in Montreal or drop to our knees and send you to paradise in a dark corner of Duqusnoy in Brussels. You pass us the rock on basketball courts in Williamsburg and cheer us when we score the winning touchdown. We can scoot our boots as deftly as we pop and lock. We have the ear of the president. We defend you against terrorists. We direct the choir and we'll keep you singing in the pew all night until you hit that high C. We take your child's hand and lead him into manhood. We die in foreign lands to defend this nation and

What Color Is Your Hoodie?

lift our voices in protest when it errs. Ours is the first face you will ever see and the last hand you will ever hold. We are sons forever in search of fathers. We are fathers without children. We make survival seem so easy yet for us survival is an act of revolt.

Indeed, we are revolutionaries. To love and allow oneself to be loved in every conceivable way, in a culture that perverts and negates love and loving relationships between racial and sexual minorities, demands that one possess the bravery to expose love and the fortitude to guard it from the scourge of oppressive forces. They are tenacious and crafty but so are we. When we kiss one another the culture quakes; beneath the earth, white men shudder in their death-sleep; the venomous tongues of Christian moralists burn to ash. Our fierce community exercises strength through fraternity. Even when we battle one another, scatter into the void, we inevitably migrate back to our mutual point of origin: this sheltering blackness, this indestructible fortress. The battles we wage against homophobia and white supremacy compel each of us to action. We shall not remain silent in the presence of injustice.

So often the stories the public hears about black gay men are tragic. HIV/AIDS rates, domestic violence, homelessness, mental health issues—these are the thoughts that typically come to mind when black gay men make themselves known to the dominant culture. Yet we are more than our struggles; we are not, should not, be defined by them. The world sees what it wants to see and if it chooses not to see us for our success then it is up to us to recognize each other and make ourselves known. Black culture, gay culture, and black gay culture invite every man who identifies as black and gay to glory in sterling histories and further the great work our forbears accomplished by resisting death and refusing to be silent. We have no right to ask for death.

Look at yourself. Go on, look. Absorb every part of yourself: your chewed up fingernails, your dreadlocks, those bee stung lips and the gap between your teeth that makes you look just like your grandmother. This is your chest, so broad, deep, and hairy. This is the birthmark your late aunt always called a strawberry and the dark blotches on your hip that just appeared one day when you were five and never went away. Do you recognize your muscular thighs and the errant gray hair on your abdomen? This can't be anyone else's skin but yours, so deliciously dark it truly does look like chocolate. This, too, is your skin, what your drunk uncle used to call piss color. The slope of your back and the rise of your ass is the best part of you you cannot see. But we love you for it because it is ours too. We maintain our indestructible bonds because we know that the most powerful words a person can hear, the most eloquent sentence one man can utter to another, is laughably simplistic yet powerful enough to dismantle centuries of injustice. It is the clarion call you answered as a boy playing hide and seek and peek-a-boo; the prayer you whisper on bended knees; the love song you wish someone would croon in your ear; the words that seal our bond: I see you.

Acknowledgments

I have many good friends to thank for lending their support to the completion of this project: Samuel Altman, Phil Anderson, Braden Berkey, Ruth Boyd-Galezewski, Andrew Breen, James Britt, Michael Buccola, Jameson Currier, Jonathan Dean, Patrick Dunn, Merry Edmondson, Ramzi Fawaz, Amy Friedman, Steven G. Fullwood, James Galezewski, Sharman Galezewski, Terri Griffith, Donovan Gwinner, Trey Hall, Lewis Hamer, Denise Hatcher, Kevin Hatcher, Nicholas Alexander Hayes, Dan Hipp, Julie Hipp, Darren Hoard, Lee James, Patrick James, James Kao, Aly Kassam-Remtulla, James Kessler, Henry Kronner, Teo Limosnero, Jeffery Lodermeier, Myrna Lovejoy, Gregory Mack, Sandy Marchetti, André Meeks, Michael Meyer, Mike Mitchell, Maria Montaño, Mimi Ojaghi, Isaac Persley, Evan Plummer, Mark Plummer, Brad Potts, Travis Ramage, John Reed, Mark Robinson, Heidi Rosenberg, George Roth, Harrison Sherrod, Tiffany Nicole Slade, Charles Stephens, Barbara Strassberg, Jay Thomas, Mark Thomas, Tony Valenzuela, Ellery Washington, Charles Wilson, Darrell Wilson, Lynn Woolfolk, and Mark Zelman.

Teachers seldom get the credit they deserve. I am lucky enough to know several who deserve special thanks: Mamie Hayman, Patricia Lyons, and Sharon Tuley were my high school English teachers and each of them encouraged my interest in literature and writing. I will be forever grateful to them for sparking my love of the written word.

During my undergraduate education at Northwestern University, Kevin Bell, Matthew Frankel, Pam Harkins, and Bill Savage taught me how to read literature critically. Thank you each for teaching me to read between the lines.

I owe enormous thanks to Sara Levine and Janet Desaulniers for taking me under their wings during my years at the School of the Art Institute of Chicago. My writing is all the better for their mentoring.

A very special thanks to my dear friend Amy Danzer for her ardent support and unwavering confidence in my writing. I'll never let you go.

Lots of love to my families: the Neals, the Piggies, and the Butters.

I cherish my parents, Debra Dunn and Brian Piggie, more than words can say. Thank you for your love, guidance, and sacrifice.

Finally, I'd like to thank my husband Gerald. Everything good in my life begins with you, Egghead.

About the Author

Jarrett Neal earned a BA in English from Northwestern University and an MFA in Writing from the School of the Art Institute of Chicago. His fiction, poetry, and essays have appeared in *Chelsea Station, The Gay and Lesbian Review, Requited Journal, The Good Men Project,* and other publications, including the Lambda Literary Award-nominated anthologies *For Colored Boys Who Have Considered Suicide When the Rainbow Is Still Not Enough* and *Black Gay Genius: Answering Joseph Beam's Call.* He lives in Oak Park, IL.

CPSIA information can be obtained
at www.ICGtesting.com
Printed in the USA
LVHW041546100521
687006LV00009B/1636